REMEMBERED

REMEDIES

of

NORTHUMBERLAND

by

Anne Larvin
BA, BSc., MBA
MNIMH

ISBN 978-1-904499-25-1

Every effort has been made to ensure that the information contained in
this book is complete and accurate. However, it is not intended to provide
professional advice or recommendation to the individual reader, nor as a
substitute for consulting a healthcare professional.

Further copies of this book may be obtained from
anne.larvin@bondgatehouse.co.uk

roundtuit
publishing

First published in the UK in 2008 by
Roundtuit Publishing, 32 Cookes Wood,
Broompark, Durham DH7 7RL

Printed in the UK by Northumbria Graphics
Northumbria University, Newcastle upon Tyne NE1 8ST

REMEMBERED
REMEDIES
of
NORTHUMBERLAND

FOREWORD

In the beginning there was a request; this became a conversation which turned into a meeting. This, in turn, became a consultation, and as information cascaded out into our County, a fully blown project involving us all. It has been written to celebrate the 90th anniversary of the formation of the Federation of Northumberland WIs.

Without the guidance and expertise of Anne, we would not have this lovely book. In its own right it is bright and attractive, full of fascinating facts but more importantly, it is a record of social history lived by women in Northumberland.

Please enjoy it, we are proud to have made it.

J.M. Wylie
Federation Chairman

ACKNOWLEDGEMENTS

I would like to thank all the members of the Northumberland WIs who gave their time and memories which are the basis of this book. It is based on both oral and written reminiscences from the members, as well as printed and handwritten books that members have in their possession which were loaned for the purposes of writing this book.

The driving force behind it and the person who saw the potential in recording these memories is Jackie Wylie—without her, this book would not have been written.

My thanks also go to the artists who have created such delightful paintings and drawings, which lift the written word and improve it beyond measure—Judith Taylor, Barbara Jobling, and Janet Jackson.

Finally, to Dr Brian Moffat who spent an afternoon on a windswept hill at Soutra Aisle, talking to me about the medieval hospital there; also to Susie White of Chesters Walled Garden for her input and expert knowledge of plants; and to Anne Stamper, the National Federation archivist for her information on the role of the WI in collecting herbs during the war.

REMEMBERED REMEDIES
of NORTHUMBERLAND

(OUR HERBAL HERITAGE)

CONTENTS

INTRODUCTION

This book originated from a desire to capture memories of how we treated health in the home and local community in the days before mass medicines, when women (often by necessity) had to use readily available remedies such as plants to treat illnesses.

In the days before over-the-counter medicines, plants were the medicines of the day—the equivalent of modern day pharmaceuticals. Even now, many of our drugs are derived from plants. However, in the course of researching and compiling this book, it has become clear just how much knowledge of local plant remedies and confidence in using them has been lost over many decades.

There is, though, a growing renewal of interest in these traditional medicines. It is easy to become confused with the bewildering array and sources of, sometimes contradictory, information. What is heartening is the way that several of these 'old wives tales' are being vindicated and validated by modern science, whilst other remedies are being investigated for new uses, such as rose hips to treat arthritis.

None of the treatments mentioned in this book is intended to replace treatment by a healthcare professional. Plants can be as powerful as modern medicines and should always be treated with respect. In the same way that some foods do not suit everyone, certain herbs can disagree with some people. Herbs are very subtle in the way they work and, depending on the dose used, can give different effects. For example rhubarb is generally considered as a laxative, but in small doses it can help to reduce diarrhoea. If in doubt about the use of a herb, you should always seek the advice of a professional herbalist. If you are already taking medication or have a continuing health problem, then you should always seek professional advice before treating yourself.

One must equally be careful of collecting plants in the wild. Some, such as eyebright, are becoming nationally endangered; others may require permission before collecting. It is also essential to ensure correct identification of a plant before using it.

I hope that as people read this book, it will stimulate interest and more memories.

WOMEN AND HEALTH

Within the home, it has (almost) always been the woman's role to look after the health of the household and treat many of the ailments that come and go. In the days before the NHS, doctors would have been expensive and, in some areas, scarce. Chemists and Druggists were important parts of many communities, and before them, Apothecaries fulfilled that role. Blacksmiths lived and worked in most communities and offered services such as tooth-pulling and basic surgery alongside their metal working. But there was always an essential core of information passed down from mother to daughter and within families on treating various maladies. Some of these treatments would have been based on 'family recipes', some from newspaper cuttings or books, and some from talking and exchange of treatments within the local community.

Centuries earlier, monasteries and their hospitals would also have been a source of information and treatments. Thropton still boasts a road called 'Physic Lane' which is reputed to be where the local monks collected herbs for their food and medicines. It would be surprising if the local people did not do the same.

The knowledge of what treatments to use, how and when was more often than not absorbed by example. Older children would pass on plant lore to younger children, sometimes as part of games and play. Members of Cambo WI remember sucking the flower heads of clover, and chewing 'sour docken' before spitting it out.

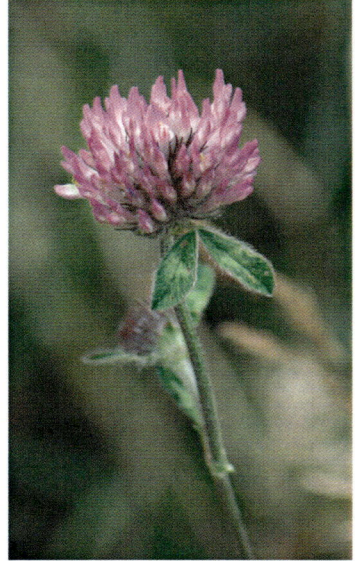

The 'Still Room' was the woman's domain where plants and herbs would be turned into medicines, creams and ointments and then stored. Drying and preserving of herbs and foods for the winter was an important task for the housewife in the days before freezers, internet shopping and supermarkets.

Women have always had a central, but often unsung, role in looking after health. Whilst the professions were largely closed to women until the middle of the nineteenth century, midwives and local women healers were always around, dispensing medicines and other treatments.

Many of these women acted as doctors or apothecaries in all but title, treating illness and dispensing medicines — without the protection of the profession or the law. Many were known as 'empirics' since much of their knowledge was based on experience. Persecution, imprisonment and fines were common for such women. But this was better than the fate that fell on some healers who were denounced as witches.

Superstition and fear, magic and incantations have always surrounded some of the traditional treatments of the distant past. It was an easy step to cry witchcraft if a treatment did not work or if there was an argument over payment. In 1649, a witch finder was hired by the town of Newcastle to seek out witches. Since he was paid by results (twenty shillings a head), it is no surprise that he was able to identify fourteen witches from the town and one witch from Chatton — a certain Jane Martin, the miller's wife. They were all executed on the Town Moor in 1650. The witch finder then went into Northumberland, where he was paid three pounds for each witch he identified. Soon after this he was imprisoned in Scotland and 'upon the gallows, he confessed he had been the death of above two hundred and twenty women in England and Scotland, for the gain of twenty shillings a-piece'.

Many of the remedies given by the members of Northumberland

WIs are what have been traditionally called 'simples'. This means that just one plant was used as the medicine, rather than several. This was a hallmark of home remedies—the simplicity of preparation and usage, as well as the availability of the plant material.

Another interesting aspect of the home remedies is the way that, for several of them, scientific interest is starting to explore and vindicate their medicinal uses and, in some cases, show new therapeutic uses. Examples of this include honey, cabbage, spider webs, rose hips and cod liver oil.

Books and pamphlets were loaned by WI members for the purposes of this book,. One pamphlet from the nineteenth or early twentieth century includes recipes for a range of patented medicines to be made at home. Being patented medicines, the exact formulae were not available, so each recipe is prefaced by the words 'approximate analysis'. The pamphlet has delightful recipes such as 'Bile Beans', 'Atkinson's Infant Preservative' and 'Dr. William's Pink Pills'. It was loaned by a member of Longhoughton & Boulmer WI.

Another fascinating book belonging to a member of Berwick WI was an Herbal originally written by Sir John Hill around the middle of the 18th century. The book belonged to the member's mother and is well thumbed. It is a charming book and excerpts from it are included in later sections. Sir John Hill (c1716-1775) worked with Linnaeus and brought the, then, new Linnaean plant classification system to this country, introduced through a book in 26 volumes entitled 'The Vegetable System'. Although he apparently qualified as a medical doctor in Edinburgh, Sir John had eclectic tastes and worked as an apothecary, writer and actor. He was obviously a controversial figure in his day, sufficient for Garrick to write a clever but cruel epigram: 'For physic and farces his equal there scarce is; his farces are physic; his physic a farce is'. His reputation has improved over recent years and he has even been described as a renaissance man, given his interests and multi-faceted talents.

Other recipes come from handwritten books kept by members' mothers or grandmothers and it is exciting to imagine them making up some of the medicines described, such as 'Strengthening Medicine' or 'A Cure for Rheumatism, Kidney and Bladder Trouble'.

WOMEN AT WAR

Many of today's powerful medicines developed from simple home remedies. Dr. William Withering in the late 18th century heard of a country cure for dropsy* 'long kept a secret by an old woman in Shropshire'. The active ingredient in this cure was found to be foxglove, and from this developed the drug digoxin (from digitalis).

Mrs J Taylor

FOX GLOVE

JT

After this, more and more plants were studied to find the 'active' ingredient and to isolate this part of the plant to produce a standardised medicine. By the time the second world war started, many essential medicines were produced in this way. Synthetic preparations had not yet arrived and plants were still the basis from which most of these medicines were derived. Unfortunately, many of the plants and plant-derived medicines were imported.

* Dropsy was an old fashioned name often used for a failing heart

For example, sparteine sulphate from the broom plant was used as a diuretic and to reduce blood pressure but it was obtained mainly from Germany. This situation made it an urgent priority both to grow more medicinal herbs in this country and also to harvest the rich variety of wild plants growing here.

In the early days of the war, the government, through the Ministry of Supply and Royal Botanic Gardens at Kew, set up the Vegetable Drugs Committee with the involvement of the Pharmaceutical Society and herb growers and traders. The Vegetable Drugs Committee drew up a list of essential plants that could be and needed to be sourced in the UK, and the help of the National Federation of WIs was sought early in the war to help with this collection. They, in turn, involved school children, Scouts and Guides in this huge undertaking.

To simplify organisation and collection, and because of the numbers of different herbs required, it was decided that 10 plants only should be collected by each county or area. Rose hip collection, which fell within this programme was not, however, limited in this way.

The setting up and running of such a scheme required an enormous amount of organisational work and skill. The County Federations worked with County Herb Committees from 1941 to organise the collection, drying and storage of medicinal plants.

Correct identification of the plants was essential—collecting hemlock instead of, say, yarrow would be fatal. Training was offered by various organisations such as the Botany departments of Universities and Colleges (including Sunderland Technical College) and speakers visited WIs to give talks and demonstrations.

Advice was given on the best times to collect different herbs: for nettles, collect the whole herb when young, and only the leaves when the stems are woody; for comfrey, collect the leaves from May onwards and the roots in autumn; for dandelion, collect the leaves from May to September and the roots in autumn and winter, and so on.

Most of the companies processing the herbs required dried herbs and it was this, together with the quantities needed that proved the biggest obstacle.

As one herb farm in Shrewsbury wrote 'hundreds of tons are required, not a few pounds. Nettle, for instance: 1000 tons of fresh [plant] would be necessary to give the 100 tons asked for and even if 1000 bodies dry them, each would have to do 1 ton'. To overcome this, WIs set up drying centres and a variety of methods were employed in the drying itself. The nearest drying centre for Northumberland WIs was however in Yorkshire, which may explain the smaller input from Northumberland (with the exception of Rosehips).

For some herbs, such as eyebright, it would have been a difficult feat to collect the required minimum of 7lbs dried weight, which would equate to around 35lbs of fresh herb. Other plants, such as comfrey leaf and elderflowers needed very careful handling to prevent damage or decay, whilst others such as berries were more robust.

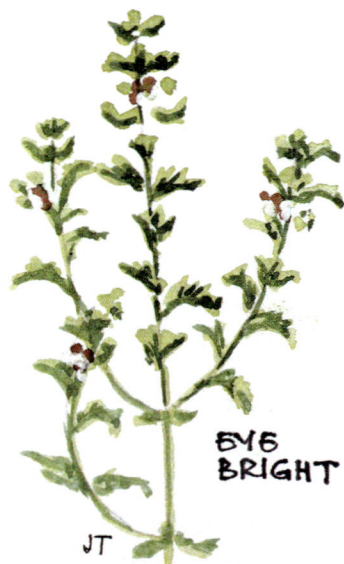

EYE BRIGHT

JT

Mrs J Taylor

The herb companies paid for all dried herbs sent to them at varying rates depending on the herb and which part of it was sent. For example foxglove leaves were paid at 1/4d per lb, but the seeds at 7/6d per lb; marigold petals, red poppy petals and red rose petals each commanded 1/9d per lb. The more 'lowly' herbs such as nettle, yarrow, mugwort and wild carrot only paid between 4d and 6d per lb.

The success of this programme can be seen in the figures. Through school children, scouts and guides, 1000 tons (1 million Kgs) of plants were gathered in 1942, which rose the following year to 2000 tons. By 1944 the target was set at 4000 tons. This collection work helped to keep vital medical supplies available during the war years

Mrs J Taylor

FOOD AS MEDICINE

Many of the home remedies given by WI members are based on foods that were readily available in the kitchen—cabbage, swede, turnip, onion, honey, vinegar, bread… Whilst the remedies using these kitchen staples focus on their medicinal use within the home, including them as part of the daily diet also provided health benefits.

Centuries ago, gardens for most people were not places of leisure, but somewhere to grow herbs and vegetables for eating and medicine as well as to keep animals for food. Food stores would be augmented by purchase and barter and by what could be gathered from the wild. Herbs and spices were important to add flavour to a staple diet that, for many, was based on bread, cereals and ale.

In the days before intensive farming and urbanisation, many more people would have had easy access to countryside to forage for food—leaves and shoots in the Spring; flowers and leaves in the Summer; fruits, seeds and nuts in the Autumn; and roots in the Winter.

Knowing which plants to collect, which parts of them to use and where they grew was passed from generation to generation. One member from Haydon Bridge WI remembers her grandmother teaching her how to identify and collect wild sorrel leaves. Spring was an important time for improving the family's diet after the winter. New leaves and shoots were excellent sources of nutrition, full of vitamins and minerals which would probably have become depleted in the diet during the winter. From this came recipes and traditions such as Easter (or Easter ledge) pudding which comprised various young green leaves mixed with onions and barley or oatmeal.

Mrs J Taylor

The leaves would more often than not include bistort, nettle and wild sorrel which are all excellent 'tonic' foods, packed full of essential nutrients. Recipes would vary from area to area, and using those plants most readily available. Herbs such as wild thyme, and hedge mustard would be used to give additional flavour. Such puddings were not only highly nutritious tonics, but also useful internal cleansers acting as diuretics and laxatives.

During the war, information was given by the Ministry of Supply about collecting and using native herbs and spices in the absence of imported products. Included in this advice was tansy (leaf) to take the place of nutmeg and cinnamon. Tansy was commonly used in the past to make the rather bitter tansy cakes which were eaten during Lent; salad burnet leaves to take the place of cucumber; the fruit of alexanders to flavour soups and stews, or the leaves and shoots eaten in place of celery.

Flowers such as borage, lavender, cowslip, rose, were used as food, medicine and decoration. Marigold flowers gave added colour to cheese and butter and a peppery taste to stews and soups.

Sweet Violet flowers were eaten as a cure for 'heart straitness' and an inflamed liver.

The leaves of sweet cicely are still used by a member of Glanton WI as an alternative to sugar to sweeten food. The leaves have a sweet, aniseed flavour and can be used cooked, fresh or dried. As well as being a food, sweet cicely has medicinal uses too, acting as a gentle stimulant to the stomach and being useful in the treatment of coughs.

SWEET VIOLET

JT

Mrs J Taylor

Herbs such as thyme, wild garlic and fennel were used to prevent or treat digestive upsets caused by 'bad' food as much as to add flavour to bland foods. Fruit vinegar poured onto Yorkshire puddings was a popular dish for some members as children. The medicinal properties of vinegar are wide and it is an excellent medium for preserving fruit and herbs. In this way, one could receive medicine, without even realising it.

Children would often nibble hedgerow plants when out. Many members recall eating 'bread and cheese' when young, not realising that the hawthorn flowers and leaves they chewed had some excellent medicinal properties for the heart and cardiovascular system.

HAW THORN

Mrs J Taylor

Home grown vegetables were a necessity for many either due to the cost of buying them or their availability, as in the war. In the past, parts of vegetables that we now consider as waste were often used. For example, the leaves of radishes are slightly spicy and were used in salads as a salad green or cooked, like spinach.

The link between nutrition and health is receiving renewed interest. However, how many people eating the recommended portions of fruit and vegetables a day are aware of the nutritional depletion food has suffered since the 1940s? In 1940, the Ministry of Agriculture published mineral and vitamin assays of a range of staple fruit and vegetables, dairy products and meat.

This work was carried on throughout the remainder of the century. By 1991, a comparison showed that the levels of macronutrients (such as sodium, potassium, magnesium, calcium and iron) had fallen significantly, as had the micronutrients, such as zinc and copper. For example, carrots in 1991 had 75% less magnesium and copper, 48% less calcium, and 46% less iron than carrots in the 1940s. A similar, though not so dramatic fall, was apparent for fruit and meat. More recently the return of diseases such as rickets, which are related to nutritional deficiencies, underlines the wisdom of earlier treatments such as cod liver oil. Many members remember with distaste their daily dose of this oil in childhood. But it ensured their levels of Vitamins A and D remained high during the winter, to strengthen their bones and immune systems.

REMEMBERED REMEDIES

In Remembered Remedies, we will see what has been used
in the past (and, in some cases, in the present) for treating a
range of illnesses. All the remedies included in this section
were given by members of the Northumberland WI, and I
am very grateful for their time, effort and care in passing on
these memories.

Treatments will be looked at under various headings, but
several of the remedies cross these artificial boundaries
and appear several times with different uses.

Infections

First Aid

Treatments for the joints

Digestive treatments

Cleansers and Tonics

Miscellaneous Remedies for
Eyes, Skin, Hair, Headaches, Women's remedies,
Kidney and Bladder treatments, Insomnia

INFECTIONS

Coughs and colds, catarrh and chest infections have been with us since time immemorial. In the past, a cough would be a matter of concern, especially if the patient had an outdoor job. The fear of developing tuberculosis was strong as it was an extremely common disease up to and into the twentieth century. Even illnesses such as pleurisy, pneumonia or whooping cough would have been treated at home, often without a doctor, either from lack of professional treatment being available or affordable, or from past experience of successful treatment.

Given the prevalence of coughs, colds, sore throats and catarrh, it is not surprising that home treatments for these conditions produced the widest range of remedies, including both internal and external treatments, and focussing very much on products readily available in the home, especially the kitchen.

In this section we will look at:

Treatments for Chest Problems, Coughs and Cold;

Earache; Catarrh and Sinus Problems; and

Treatments for Sore Throats

CHEST INFECTIONS, COUGHS & COLDS

Vegetables were a readily available source of medicine in the home. Four vegetables feature in these remedies—onion, turnip, swede and garlic—for chesty coughs and colds.

Onions were used for a wide range of respiratory problems both as a preventive and as a treatment. Versatile, and effective, onions could even be called a 'super medicine'.

Onion Syrup/Onion Juice

Used variously for chesty coughs, colds, and as a preventive by Humshaugh, Alnwick, Warkworth and Norham WIs:

The basic recipe for **onion syrup** involves sprinkling sugar (either white or Demerara) onto a cut onion, leaving for a period until a juice has formed. Decant the juice and drink.

A variation on this basic remedy was given by Riding Mill WI as follows:

Use Spanish onions and brown sugar, and for this to be left in front of an open fire to allow a syrup to form.

Other uses of Onion

Raw, sliced onions, applied to the feet, for a cold.

Pobs, comprising white bread, milk and onions, cooked together and eaten, for colds.

Half a cut onion in the room where there was infection.

Boiled onions. As a preventive against colds, once a week, eat the onions and drink the liquor.

Turnip syrup for coughs

This was a remedy given by both Acomb and Berwick WIs: Cut a turnip in half and scoop out some flesh. Add sugar to the flesh and then leave, covered, until a syrup forms. Drink the syrup.

Swede Syrup for bronchitis

Cook and mash a swede and then mix with black treacle. Take as large a dose as possible at night. (Humshaugh WI)

Mrs J Taylor

Mashed swede & black treacle.

Liquorice, Garlic and Honey was used to treat chesty coughs by a member of Warkworth WI. How this was prepared as a medicine we do not know. Home preparation would probably involve a decoction of liquorice root, with the juice of garlic added and then sweetened with honey. Liquorice has been used for chesty coughs since the Middle Ages. It has an anti-inflammatory effect to soothe chest inflammation as well as anti-viral properties. Both garlic and honey have antiseptic activity to treat infection.

Ginger and Beer boiled together as a drink was a home remedy given by Acomb WI. This would provide a calming, soothing drink for a patient with an irritable cough, since hops (in beer) are often used to help insomnia, and ginger is a gently warming, anti-emetic herb.

Thyme herb was also used to make cough mixtures by WI members. Thyme grows wild in parts of Northumberland, especially along the coast, but is more commonly known as a garden herb for adding flavour to dishes. It has been used for centuries for this purpose, but also as an antiseptic herb to reduce or eliminate problems associated with 'tainted' meats, particularly in the Middle Ages. It is thyme's antiseptic properties that make it such an excellent herb for treating chesty coughs.

Thyme Cough Mixture

2oz. Thyme in a teapot, pour boiling water over,

as for making tea.

Infuse for 10 minutes, strain into a pan.

Add 300gms honey and 300gms sugar.

Heat gently to dissolve, then stir and simmer until slightly

thickened. Skim off the 'scum' and allow to cool.

Bottle in dark bottles and refrigerate.

Fruits formed the basis of some of the home remedies for coughs and colds, whether as syrups or vinegars or infusions:

Blackcurrant jam dissolved in boiling water would make a pleasant tasting syrup for colds. Packed full of Vitamin C, this is a valuable support for the immune system as well as having some anti-viral properties. In the early days of the war, blackcurrant syrup was used instead of rose hip syrup for its vitamin content, before it was realised that rose hips contained even more Vitamin C.

Lemon juice was a popular home remedy in drinks for colds and sore throats. As with blackcurrant jam, it is lemon's Vitamin C content in the juice that makes this remedy effective. Lemon juice is valuable as a cooling drink in fevers or whenever the temperature is raised.

A very traditional treatment, especially for lung infections, was the use of poultices and plasters. This was a treatment used both in the home, and by doctors.

A **Linseed** poultice was an effective treatment for congested lungs in such cases as bronchitis, pneumonia or pleurisy. It makes a very soothing remedy, especially for pain and inflammation. (Old Hartley WI)

Bread poultices were also used for chesty condition. One WI specifically mentioned using this on the back as a cure for pleurisy. (Bolam Park WI)

A **Mustard** plaster was also popular for chest infections. Very similar to a poultice, a mustard plaster draws blood to the surface of the skin, and so helps relieve internal inflammation and congested lungs. (Norham WI)

Bread would sometimes be mixed with the mustard powder to make a plaster, which would both increase the 'drawing' action and reduce the chance of irritating or burning the skin, as can happen with mustard. (Berwick WI)

Other external treatments for chest problems included:

Goose fat or **Goose grease**. In one case, the goose fat was rubbed onto the chest and then covered with brown paper, for chesty colds; and another use called for goose grease mixed with camphorated oil to be rubbed onto the chest for bronchial ills.

Red Flannel was also used as a wrap over goose grease, for both chest infections and sore throats. Whilst flannel is a warm material, it is the colour that is important in this treatment. Colours have long been thought to have different therapeutic effects. In Ayurvedic (Traditional Indian) medicine, the colour red is thought to stimulate the immune system and improve the circulation. More recent research is looking at the physiological and psychological effects of colour and finding, for example, that red improves concentration and even that there is a perceived difference in the effects of drugs, depending on their colour.

WHOOPING COUGH

Whooping cough was, at one time, an exceptionally common infection in children, and often fatal if the child was less than a year old. Since the introduction of the pertussis vaccine, occurrence has reduced but not been eliminated.

One remedy given to a member of Berwick WI by a gypsy over fifty years ago involved **saltpetre and blotting paper**. A two inch square of blotting paper should be soaked in saltpetre and then set alight in the room of the patient.

Another remedy given for whooping cough was the following recipe:

For Whooping Cough

1 gill White Vinegar

2 pennyworth of Barley Sugar

2 pennyworth of Honey

1 Fresh Egg

½lb Lump Sugar

Beat together and bottle. Dose 2 or 3 teaspoonfuls.

(Miss L Alexander, Old Hartley WI)

From a handwritten notebook and dated 6th April 1873

Cough Mixture

¼ lb of Honey

1oz. Sweet Nitre

1oz Paregoric*

1 pint boiling water

Mix all together and bottle for use.

(Corbridge WI)

And another recipe...

Cough Mixture

2 pennyworth of Paregoric*

2 pennyworth of Laudanum**

2 pennyworth of Oil of Aniseed

2 pennyworth of Oil of Peppermint

1lb Black Treacle

1 pint Boiling Water

Dissolve the treacle with the boiling water. When nearly
cold, add the mixture and bottle.

(*Paregoric is camphorated opium; **Laudanum is opium)

EARACHE

Two WIs mentioned using **onions for earache**. An onion would be boiled until soft, and then the warm core would be placed inside the ear. The warmth of the onion would be soothing, and the juice of the cooked onion would act as an antibiotic. This treatment could be used for both children and adults.

Mrs J Jackson

CATARRH AND SINUS PROBLEMS

Camphor, either as an oil or as camphor balls, was mentioned by several WIs to treat catarrh and sinus problems, as well as colds. Old Hartley, Ulgham, and Bolam Park WIs each had a slightly different use: camphor balls in a bag were hung round the neck for a bad chest, or a cold; the oil was rubbed into the chest if there was a chesty cough or nasal catarrh.

Radishes were mentioned by Cambo WI, to be eaten as a specific remedy to reduce nasal catarrh.

For blocked sinuses, **garlic and honey**, mixed together and placed up the nostrils would help to clear the nasal passages. A word of caution: raw garlic placed directly onto the skin or any mucous membrane (such as the lining of the nose) can cause blistering and burning if the skin is very sensitive, or if left in place too long.

Mrs J Taylor

GARLIC & HONEY.

SORE THROATS

Black Bullets

This traditional North East mint sweet was created in 1906 in Newcastle. Made from peppermint oil, sugar, glucose and water, the story goes that that it took its name from the moulds used to make musket balls.

Riding Mill and Cambo WIs mentioned syrups made from Black Bullets:

Steep the Black Bullets in vinegar for a few days until a syrup is formed. Drink the syrup for both sore throats and chesty coughs.

For a more luxurious treatment from Bolam Park WI: Dissolve the Black Bullets in a little rum and honey. Drink the resulting liquor for coughs.

Mrs J Taylor

Black bullets in rum & honey.

In the same way that vegetable juices and syrups were used for chesty coughs and colds, fruits provided popular treatments for sore throats, as well as for coughs and colds too. The fruit, in the form of a vinegar or a syrup, would be used either as a gargle or a drink.

Fruit Vinegars: Raspberry vinegar, blackberry vinegar and a raspberry, blackberry and blackcurrant vinegar were all mentioned for treating sore throats. The fruit vinegar would be added to hot water and the liquid either drunk, or gargled.

Vinegar was also used on its own in remedies given by Old Hartley WI and Ulgham WI. Mixed with butter and sugar (possibly to make it more palatable), vinegar was used for treating sore throats and colds.

Blackcurrant syrup was given to children who were suffering from sore throats.

Onion juice in honey was another childhood memory, used when the throat was sore. The onion juice is antiseptic, and the honey would add its own antiseptic activity as well as soothing a sore throat

Cayenne pepper

A remedy to treat sore throats was given by Mrs Taylor of Humshaugh WI. It involved placing some cayenne pepper onto a spoon handle and then very gently dropping the cayenne pepper down the back of the throat.

Cayenne is the ground, dried fruit of the capsicum plant, and the fresh fruit is called a chilli pepper. The plant gets its name from the Greek word—*Kapto*—I bite, and it is indeed hot and pungent. When taken in excess it can cause very painful burning, especially if any juice gets into the eyes!

Cayenne is a very old, traditional remedy for sore throats and tonsillitis—usually included with other herbs or foods, to reduce the fierceness of its heat.

CAYENNE PEPPER DOWN THE THROAT!

Mrs J Taylor

Cayenne Pepper continued.

Its medicinal properties include acting as a powerful internal 'disinfectant' especially in the digestive tract, as well as being an excellent warming herb to improve the circulation, particularly to cold hands and feet.

Its stimulating and warming properties have meant that it has often been used in the past as a plaster or poultice for joints and muscles, to both relieve inflammation and reduce pain. Indeed, recent hospital trials have shown it to be an effective analgesic, reducing the amount of morphine required after surgery, for both adults and children.

ONIONS

Onions belong to the same family as leeks and garlic, all containing similar chemical constituents, to a greater or lesser degree. Onions have always been a traditional home remedy—not least because they are readily available. Cooked or raw, they offered a wide range of treatments, from gallstones and dropsy, to chilblains and asthma. They have even been used externally to rub onto stings. Like garlic, onions are both antiseptic and also help lower blood cholesterol. A member of Norham WI also remembers the use of boiled onions to help 'the nerves'.

For respiratory problems, onions have a long-standing reputation for helping to loosen and clear thick, congested catarrh whether in the head, sinuses or lungs. As Culpeper wrote, 'being roasted...and eaten with honey or sugar and oil, they [help] relieve an inveterate cough and expectorate tough phlegm'. Although he did say that they are 'flatulent and windy' yet 'they somewhat promote the appetite'. John Gerard, writing some 60 years earlier in 1597, said that ' the juice sniffed up into the nose, purgeth the head and draweth forth raw, phlegmaticke humours' - it would certainly make your eyes water!

MUSTARD

Probably brought to Britain by the Romans, mustard has been used here as a condiment and medicine since then. St Bede, in his writings, talks of using mustard for colds in the head. It is a hot, pungent plant and mustard poultices draw blood to the skin's surface and so help relieve internal inflammation and congested lungs. A hot water footbath with mustard powder can help raise body temperature, increase blood circulation and generally stimulate the body to throw off a cold and relieve catarrhal congestion. Care must always be used when placing mustard directly onto the skin or mucous membranes as it can burn and cause blistering.

LINSEED

Flaxseed (linseed, from linen-seed), has been cultivated for millennia for its use in cloth-making and as a medicine. A poultice is extremely soothing in chest infections such as pleurisy and pneumonia, where there is inflammation and pain. It has traditionally been used as a tea for coughs, sore throats and croup because of its moistening and soothing action. The seeds contain significant amounts of omega 3 essential fatty acids, important as an anti-inflammatory agent in the body.

SWEDE AND TURNIP

Both swede and turnip are brassicas and members of the Cruciferae (Mustard) family. Like all vegetables, they contain vitamins, especially Vitamin C, and minerals such as calcium, potassium, manganese and phosphorus—all essential contributors to our health. However, their medicinal activity most probably comes from other constituents, known as glucosinolates, which are sulphur-based chemicals present in all members of the mustard family. Glucosinolates irritate the skin and can cause inflammation, and it is this counter irritation effect that provides the medicinal effect when used externally. Glucosinolates inhibit the function of the thyroid gland, and eating a lot of raw vegetables from the brassica family is not recommended for those with low thyroid function.

BLACK TREACLE

The origin of the name 'treacle' comes from the Latin '*theriaca*', meaning 'antidote to poison'. Black treacle is oozing with iron, so for example 35g of black treacle contains 3.2mg of iron, compared with 100gm broccoli which contains just 1 mg. This makes it an excellent food for iron-deficiency anaemia.

GARLIC

This is truly a 'wonder' medicine with many, wide-ranging health benefits. It lowers blood cholesterol, helps lower blood pressure, reduces 'stickiness' of the blood, and is an extremely powerful antibiotic (internally and externally). The active ingredient is an oil produced when a clove is crushed. This oil travels round the body in the blood and is removed through the lungs—which is why the breath smells when one uses garlic. Try rubbing a cut clove of garlic on the sole of the foot, and within 2 hours you will find your breath smells of garlic.

Garlic is one of the few herbs used extensively in each of the three great healing systems of the world—Western Herbal Medicine, Ayurveda, and Traditional Chinese Medicine.

Garlic has been a valuable medicine through the ages. In Ancient Egypt, the Ebers Codex, written in 1550 BC has 22 different medicinal formulations that included garlic.

Mrs J Jackson

RADISH

The radish takes its name for the Saxon word *rude*, meaning ruddy. Like swede and turnip, the radish contains appreciable amounts of glucosinolates which means that it was often used in the same way and for the same conditions as swede and turnip. Likewise, the same precautions apply for those with an under-active thyroid.

The root is the part of the plant now used as a food and medicine, but the young leaves and flowers were used frequently as a salad and a cooked vegetable.

Radish stimulates the appetite and has been used to expel worms in the gut. However, because of the hot, acrid oil found in the root, it is not recommended if there is inflammation or ulceration in the digestive system. A poultice of the root has traditionally been used to alleviate asthma and chest complaints and even smelly feet. (The volatile oil is both antifungal and antibacterial).

In the eighteenth century, Sir John Hill wrote ' the juice of the root freshly gathered with a little white wine is an excellent remedy against the gravel. Scarce anything operates more speedily, or brings away little stones more successfully.'

CAMPHOR

The Camphor tree is related to the Cinnamon tree. Camphor is an evergreen, growing in China and the Far East where it has long been a valuable medicine for both internal and external use. The medicinal use nowadays comes largely from the essential oil in the leaves and branches, but tinctures were popular in the West in the nineteenth century and before.

It is a common ingredient in liniments for joint and muscle pain as it has analgesic and warming properties, and it is also popular as an inhalant or chest rub to loosen catarrh in bronchial and sinus congestion.

A popular constituent in Victorian medicines was *paregoric* which is a camphorated oil of opium. In the past, the aromatic oils from tansy and feverfew have also been called camphor, which led to much confusion. Many old recipes also talk of 'camphire' - sometimes meaning camphor, sometimes henna, and occasionally true camphire.

VINEGAR

A sour liquid, made by fermentation, vinegar acts as a solvent and preservative for plants and fruits infused in it. Malt vinegar, nowadays, is usually synthetically produced and bears no relation to true vinegars of the past which were produced mainly from barley. Medicated vinegars are those with herbs such as sage or thyme, or fruits such as raspberry or blackberry infused in them. They have been used since the time of Hippocrates in 300 BC as a medicine. A true vinegar is antiseptic, promotes secretions in the body, helps to check perspiration (and so cool the body in fevers), and it soothes and cools skin irritation or inflammation caused by sunburn or itching.

Drinking apple cider vinegar is a traditional remedy for joint problems, as it helps to reduce the amount of acid in the body — a common situation in those with joint inflammation.

Mrs B Jobling

FIRST AID

First aid treatments for cuts, scrapes, burns and bruises were the mainstay of home remedies—dealing with the day-to-day accidents of adults and children. They still are, but 100 years ago antiseptic creams such as Savlon did not exist. Instead people would use plants or mineral products which had antiseptic properties. Many of the plants used in this way offered much more than simple antisepsis— they often provided other actions such as reducing inflammation and improving healing times.

As might be expected, all the treatments mentioned in this section are external remedies for cuts, bruises, burns, skin ulcers and warts, as well as 'drawing' treatments for boils, whitlows and spells.

In this section remedies are given for:

Treatments for Sprains and Strains, Bumps and Bruises; Antiseptic and Wound Healing Treatments; Drawing Remedies; and Treatments for Burns, Stings, Bites and Warts

COMFREY

Norham, Bolam Park, and Shilbottle WIs used comfrey in a range of remedies including treatments for pain and swelling, for skin ulcers and healing wounds.

For **pain and swelling**, a comfrey leaf should be placed under the bandage. **For sprains**, comfrey leaves boiled and then applied as a poultice.

For skin ulcers, apply either a comfrey leaf poultice or compress, or the area affected to be washed with comfrey leaf liquid. The leaves contain mucilage - a slimy substance which is very soothing and anti-inflammatory. Although not noted for any antiseptic properties, comfrey leaf is a powerful and fast wound healer.

An Healing Ointment

Chop comfrey leaves and mix in lard to a smooth paste.

Use to heal cuts and bruises

(Ponteland WI)

One delightful story from Norham WI told of how fishermen from Seahouses used to take fresh comfrey plants on their fishing trips into the North Sea, in the nineteenth century. Given the healing properties of comfrey, it would have made an ideal first aid remedy for those on board.

Comfrey cont...

In the past, both root and leaf have been used in treatments internally and externally. The root is the more powerful part of the plant and has the strongest traditional use, although the leaf has similar, but less powerful properties. However, the root must only be used externally as it does contain some strong alkaloid which can cause liver damage in a small number of people or if used to excess.

Comfrey shares, with a few other plants, a common name of **Knitbone**, due to its ability to speed the healing process of broken bones. This activity actually applies to all connective tissue, including ligaments, tendons and skin, as well as ulcers in the digestive tract. However, because of its speed of action and effectiveness, it is always important to ensure that there is no deep or lingering infection before using this treatment.

COMFREY LEAVES.

JT

Mrs J Taylor

SPRAINS AND STRAINS; BUMPS AND BRUISES

Other treatments for sprains and strains were:

For sprains, **Mallow leaves**, boiled and made into a poultice to apply to the affected part .

A footbath of **warm water and vinegar** for foot or ankle swelling. One WI member mentioned that the foot should be left in the footbath until the water was cold.
Alternatively, a **cloth soaked in vinegar** and applied to the affected area would help reduce swelling.

Vinegar and brown paper was used for a pain in the side: Apply vinegar to the skin and then cover with brown paper, and warm with an iron.

VINEGAR & BROWN PAPER   JT

Mrs J Taylor

Cabbage leaf was a traditional favourite for reducing swelling and mending sprains. Both Bolam Park and Norham WIs mentioned this remedy. The cabbage needed to be a dark green, the darker the better. The leaf would either be chopped up or used whole and applied to the swollen area. Dark green cabbage is the most efficacious variety.

Cod Liver Oil Cream was a remedy used on septic bruises or varicose ulcers. Research carried out in Denmark in 2000 showed that cod liver oil ointment did indeed speed wound healing. With high levels of omega 3 essential fatty acid, and Vitamins A and D, this may explain why cod liver oil cream works so effectively.

Dark green seaweed, as a poultice, was mentioned for treating strains and sprains. The seaweed was not identified, but was collected from the beach near Seaton Sluice. With over 10,000 different species worldwide, there are particular seaweeds that have a long history of medicinal use, including up to the present day. Living on an island, it is no wonder that there are many traditions surrounding certain seaweeds. The water-absorbing properties of seaweed are thought to be the reason behind their use to 'draw' boils and suppurations; the filmy texture of many native seaweeds

Dark green seaweed cont...

made it useful as a compress for nosebleeds, migraines, burns and even for laying on the abdomen after childbirth, to induce removal of the afterbirth. It does have an anti-inflammatory action too, and that may lie behind the tradition of heating seaweed and then laying onto a rheumatic knee.

One particular variety—Bladderwrack— has been used since Victorian times to aid weight loss. It works by stimulating the thyroid gland, which is responsible for the rate of our metabolism. However, this can be a very dangerous way to lose weight, as over-stimulating the thyroid gland can lead to goitre and to a condition known as hyperthyroidism. **It is not recommended for home treatment.**

ANTISEPTIC AND WOUND HEALING REMEDIES

Most of the remedies given for antisepsis and wound healing offered a range of other benefits too, which is one of the trademarks of home remedies. This is also why some of the remedies have already appeared as treatments for other problems.

Calendula infused oil was recommended for bathing wounds and cuts. Calendula (or Marigold) is a popular garden plant with intensely bright orange flowers. The flower head (or, even better, just the petals) was used as an external treatment to disinfect wounds, cuts and scrapes. The flowers would be either infused in oil or used to make an ointment, both of which would be bright orange. Calendula not only disinfects but also improves wound healing times.

The flowers have been used for centuries in creams, ointments and oils as a natural antiseptic and wound healing herb. The petals give a beautiful deep orange/ gold colour to any cream, although it does stain. The name 'marigold' is a shortened form of St. Mary's Gold, indicating how much it was revered as a monastery herb.

Calendula cont…

It has been used since at least the Middle Ages as an internal herb for digestive problems, especially to improve liver function. This has given it a reputation as a cleansing herb and this explains its modern use in treating skin conditions such as eczema. It was also traditionally used as an eyebath for inflammation or infections such as conjunctivitis.

Marigold is an excellent skin cleansing, antiseptic herb which reduces inflammation and aids healing.

Honey was mentioned as a treatment for wounds and cuts, and spread onto infected skin ulcers. Honey has been used since the time of the Egyptians to treat wounds, and has a long history of successful use to both disinfect, deodorise, speed healing and reduce scarring.

It is now being looked at again in hospitals to treat slow healing ulcers. However, honey available from the shops, is not sterile and in some people it may cause an allergic reaction to bee pollen if that is present in the honey.

Spider's Web was a remembered remedy by one member of Alnwick WI, used for wrapping around cuts and wounds to bind them up, particularly during the Second World War. A spider's web does not have any known antiseptic properties, but it provides an incredibly strong and light bandage to draw a wound together, which speeds the healing process and reduces the risk of infection. Scientists are already working on ways to genetically produce a spider 'silk' to be used in surgery and wound treatments.

Mrs J Taylor

Spider's Web cont...

Natural spider web silks are, weight for weight, six times stronger than steel, with greater tensile strength, and at least 25% lighter than any man-made materials used in wound healing. It has been calculated that a spider web silk as thick as a pencil would be strong enough to tow an ocean liner!

There is substantial folklore on the medicinal use of spiders webs to bind wounds, at least as far back as the Middle Ages, and it is highly likely that its use dates back long before this. It is an ideal first aid home remedy, although it would be important to ensure that the wound was not infected before applying the spider silk.

Cabbage leaf has appeared already as a treatment for swellings. However, it was also recommended by Alnwick WI for treating leg ulcers—as a poultice, applied to the ulcerated leg. The humble cabbage has some exceptional health properties, stimulating the local circulation to the area where the poultice is applied, which reduces swelling and speeds wound healing. The juice also acts as an effective antibiotic.

Stockholm Tar was a remedy given by Humshaugh WI, being used to stop infection in a cut or wound. The tar would be heated and applied to a scrape on a knee, elbow or hand with a rag. The tar, from the Scots Pine tree, is antibacterial and antifungal and is still sold nowadays, as a veterinary treatment for horses.

HOT STOCKHOLM TAR

Mrs J Taylor

Zambuk ointment was used on cuts and scrapes.

In 1915 it was advertised as 'quickly kills all germs, stops the bleeding, prevents suppuration and blood poison and heals quickly.' By 1945 this impressive list of actions had been toned down to ' soothes and heals that foot trouble' and 'relieves chafing, skin eruptions, cuts, burns, bruises'.

The ointment is now based on petroleum jelly, pine resin and beeswax, with eucalyptus oil, camphor and thyme oil. But below is a recipe for Zambuk from the pamphlet loaned by a member of Longhoughton & Boulmer WI:

ZAM-BUK (Approx. Formula)

White Wax   1oz

Burgundy Pitch ¼oz

Camphor ¼ oz

Borax Acid ¼ oz

Green oil of Elder ½ oz

Melt in a pot like glue, then put the pot into a basin of cold water, and stir until it sets.

DRAWING REMEDIES

Poultices to 'draw' infections from wounds, spots and boils, and to remove whitlows and spells were a very common home treatment.

A **Bread Poultice** was mentioned variously for drawing whitlows, boils and wounds. Bread would be mixed with boiling water to a paste-like consistency and then applied to the appropriate part as hot as possible. This would be wrapped on and left. Although the heat would be painful, it would draw blood to the surface of the skin - an essential part of this treatment. The wheat in the bread would draw fluid to it, helping with the treatment. In the days before modern, factory-made bread, most breads were either home made or from a local baker, without the preservatives or chemicals in our bread now. Bread may very well have contained moulds such as penicillin, which may account for the many records of successfully using bread poultices for wounds—effectively using antibiotics before they were discovered!

Two variations on the making of a bread poultice were mentioned—in one case, sugar was added (for boils); and in another, the bread was chewed rather than mixed with boiling water, and the chewed, softened bread applied as a poultice.

A Sugar and Soap Poultice to 'draw infection' was another very traditional home remedy. The soap would be grated and then mixed with sugar to a paste, before applying to a wound or boil to draw the infection to a 'head'.

SOAP & SUGAR POULTICE

Mrs J Taylor

Magnesium Sulphate Paste was another drawing paste used to draw 'spelks', boils and carbuncles . Also known as Epsom salts, it comprises not surprisingly magnesium and sulphur.

BURNS

Burns can be very serious, and are not suitable for home treatment unless they are minor burns. However, first aid treatment before medical attention is available can be important both in reducing damage and the chance of infection. The area burnt should be cooled with cold water (but not ice as this can worsen the damage), and then protected from infection. Oils such as butter and ointments can slow down the cooling process and are not recommended immediately after a burn.

Lavender oil was mentioned as being used to treat burns. This is still used as a first aid remedy for minor burns, with the essential oil easily available. Lavender water or infused oil would probably have been used in the past.

Mrs J Taylor

LAVENDER OIL

JT

A **Vinegar Wash or Compress** for sunburn was used when the skin was uncomfortable. This remedy was given by Corbridge WI. The vinegar compress would be replaced as required, with the result was that the skin did not peel. Vinegar has already been mentioned earlier for treating sore throats, but in this instance vinegar would help to cool the skin and so reduce the discomfort. This cooling effect will help reduce dehydration of the skin and so reduce the likelihood of peeling. In another context, vinegar was also given as a remedy by Ulgham WI to relieve the itch of rashes.

Cold Tea—as an eyebath when a spark from welding burnt the eye. Tea contains tannins which are astringent. and form a protective coating over the burnt area. The more tea cools, the greater the levels of tannins, which is why there is a 'puckering' sensation in the mouth when drinking cold tea.

The juice of **Houseleeks** was recommended to apply to the skin for burns, insect bites and sunburn. This is a very old remedy, having been used medicinally since Ancient Greek times to reduce inflammation in a range of ailments from shingles and neuralgia to corns, and inflamed eyes. The houseleek takes its name from the Anglo-Saxon word '*leac*' meaning a plant, so the name literally means 'house plant'.

Aloe vera juice or gel was also mentioned to spread onto burns. Whilst the plant is available for growing as an indoor plant, it would most probably have been purchased from the chemist as a gel or cream. It is increasingly popular as an effective skin treatment for inflamed and sore skin. The juice from the leaves is very soothing for burns and other skin problems. Rinsing the mouth with the juice can help bleeding or sore gums, periodontal disease and tonsillitis. Aloe vera takes its name from the Arabic word 'alloeh' meaning bitter, shiny substance. The gel and juice from the leaf is soothing and anti-inflammatory and is sometimes recommended for irritable bowel disease. The sap, however, contains a powerful laxative which can irritate the digestive system.

Honey was also mentioned as a remedy to use on burns. A newspaper cutting from around 1800 recounts the story of a lady in Rome in 1789:

> '.who had the misfortune to be severely burned over almost the whole of her body' when her clothes caught fire. 'To give temporary care, a domestic had recourse to some honey that lay at hand and which had so good an effect, that at the end of nine days, she was perfectly cured by use of this remedy alone.'

STINGS

Insect bites and stings were and are common hazards for adults and children. We often do not know what insect has bitten us until we get the reaction of swelling and itching. Stings, on the other hand, are usually felt more immediately and the culprit known.

Dock Leaf was mentioned several times as the traditional remedy for nettle stings. It is one of the few home treatments that children nowadays are aware of and use. One person mentioned spitting on the dock leaf, before rubbing into the skin. This helps the action of the dock leaf as enzymes in saliva activate chemicals in the dock leaf more quickly.

For bee stings, two treatments were given that would help to neutralise the poison in the sting.

Nettle leaf, rubbed onto the sting.

Rub the sting with a **Blue bag (Dolly bag).**

(A Blue bag was made by a company called Reckitts. It was added to the rinsing water in the days before automatic washing machines. The advertising claimed that 'it made whites, whiter than white').

BITES

Insect bites do not always happen at home or where you have a first aid cabinet easily to hand. Away from home, many plant leaves can calm an insect bite— leaves such as plantain or ribwort, yarrow and chickweed. All these plants can be used as a temporary poultice by either chewing to soften (but only if you are absolutely sure you have identified the plant correctly) or rolling between the fingers to release the sap and then applying to the bite.

Lavender oil was mentioned for treating insect stings and bites. Lavender oil was used in France during the First World War to wash wounds because of its antiseptic properties.

Epsom Salts were recommended as a treatment for midge bites, and **Baking Soda** for insect bites in general. Both these remedies would help to 'draw' out any inoculated venom and help neutralise it.

WARTS

Caused by a virus that settles into the skin, a wart is not a serious health problem, but it can feel and be unsightly. Warts can appear anywhere on the body, but the feet, hands and face are the most common sites. They are possibly the ailment for which the widest range of folk remedies exist.

Dandelion sap from the stalk was the most frequently mentioned treatment for warts. The fresh sap would be rubbed onto the wart, which would soon turn black. Repeated two or three times a day, this remedy usually worked but could take some weeks, before the wart shrank and eventually disappeared. The white latex from the stem is also present in the root and has been used traditionally for corns and verrucas as well as warts.

Mrs J Jackson

61

Spurge was also given as a remedy for warts. Spurge has been used nationwide for warts, as evidenced by some of its common names—from 'wart weed' in Cornwall, to 'warty-girse' in Orkney. The juice from the leaf or the stem would have a similar effect to that of Dandelion. It has a caustic sap which can be a severe irritant, causing photo-sensitivity and severe inflammation in contact with sensitive skin, eyes or open cuts.

One fascinating remedy given by Old Hartley WI advised that the wart be rubbed with **meat** (possibly bacon), and the meat buried in the garden. As the meat decayed, so would the wart.

Many remedies for warts were used interchangeably for corns. This recipe, from a handwritten notebook, appears on the same page as a cure for Warble Fly in cattle.

Cure for Corns and Warts

'Wash well with warm water. Steep white bread among vinegar for a poultice. Lay it on at night for two nights.'

(from a notebook belonging to
Mrs E Bramwell, Horsley WI)

REMEDIES FOR THE JOINTS

Joint and muscle pain is a centuries old problem, not only related to age, but also to the working life.

The bone setter was a familiar figure in many towns and villages in the past, who often combined work on people with that on animals (especially horses). Indeed, many of the local healers, as opposed to doctors, treated both animals and people, often with similar remedies.

Whilst only a small number of remedies were given specifically for joints and rheumatism, some of the treatments included in the First Aid section would, in all likelihood, have also been used—cabbage, and seaweed in particular. In fact, any of the treatments given for treating swellings and strains would help with joint and muscle problems.

In this section we will look at:

White Willow; Wild Carrot; Comfrey leaf; and Cabbage

For aches and pains, a member of Norham WI remembered the use of **Willow leaves.** The willow leaves were gathered and then placed down the back of the corset and left to work as a poultice on the lower back. Another member also remembers the use of a willow gel, rubbed into an aching arm.

White willow (Salix alba) has a long history of medicinal use, as far back as the Ancient Egyptians, who prepared a general purpose tonic with white willow bark, beer, figs and dates. The use of white willow continued through Greek and Roman times and is still in use in the present day. Many of the ancient treatments and most of the modern day treatments use the bark of the willow as it is believed to contain the highest concentration of therapeutic properties. But there is also historic information on the use of the leaves. The Roman doctor, Celsus, used the leaf to relieve inflammation, and Dioscorides, a hugely influential doctor in Roman times, used the soaked leaves to relieve aching body parts. In the 18th century, when malaria was very common in Europe, the bitterness of willow bark was likened to the recently discovered Cinchona tree (from which came quinine), and so willow bark became a common treatment for malaria in Europe since quinine was much more expensive and rare.

Willow cont...

White willow contains the chemical salicin which is converted in the body to salicylic acid, and has analgesic, anti-inflammatory and anti-pyretic properties. Because of its salicin content, white willow should not be used by those allergic or sensitive to aspirin. In therapeutic doses, it should only be used under professional supervision for those taking anticoagulant drugs (such as warfarin or heparin) or beta blockers (such as atenolol and propanolol) since willow may interfere with their effectiveness.

Comfrey leaf, as a poultice, has already been mentioned in the First Aid section, to treat sprains and swellings. It was also given as a remedy for aches and pains in the wrists and feet, possibly for problems such as arthritis and/or rheumatism. In this case, the leaves were wrapped around the affected area. Although comfrey leaf has no pain-relieving properties, it does help to reduce inflammation (and thereby, the pain associated with it), and to improve and strengthen the integrity of joint tissues such as cartilage and ligaments and tendons.

Cabbage leaf has also been mentioned as a first aid remedy, treating swellings and sprains. A poultice applied to arthritic joints, will have a similar anti-inflammatory effect.

Wild Carrot was the only internal remedy mentioned for treating joint problems and rheumatism. It was given by Mrs J. Taylor of Humshaugh WI. An infusion of the dried leaves was taken for 'its cleansing effect'. The only comment about its efficacy was that 'it tasted terrible'.

Wild Carrot is believed to be the forerunner of the cultivated carrot, and delights in the common name of Queen Anne's Lace. As well as the leaves, the roots and seeds have been used medicinally. The seeds were traditionally used as a 'morning after' contraceptive, since they contain chemicals which stimulate the uterus, and experiments indicate that they also reduce implantation of fertilised eggs.

WILD CARROT

JT

Mrs J Taylor

Wild Carrot cont...

The leaves were the part of the plant most commonly associated with traditional use, particularly to act as a diuretic—hence the 'cleansing effect' mentioned. Because of this strong diuretic action, it has been used for a range of kidney and bladder problems, including kidney stones and cystitis. In the case of kidney stones, it had the reputation of not only countering their formation in the first place, but also reducing stones that may have already formed. Increasing diuresis was a common way of treating joint diseases in the past, as it helped to increase elimination of uric acid from the body (often responsible for joint pain). And given its diuretic effects, it is no wonder that an infusion of the leaf was also recommended as an herb to treat dropsy.

Mrs Taylor also told of how she used to go with her grandfather to collect the plant. Her grandfather always dug the whole plant up to ensure correct identification. This was an excellent precaution since the plant can be, and has been, mistaken for some of the poisonous members of the Umbelliferae family—notably hemlock—with fatal results!

A Recipe for Rheumatism

1oz Gum Guaiacum
1oz Saltpetre
1oz White Mustard Seed
1 pint proof Rum

Mix together and bottle.
Dose one wineglass night and morning

(Recipe from Miss E Alexander,
Old Hartley WI)

Guaiacum comes from the Lignum vitae tree, a native of
the West Indies. It became a popular ingredient in many
Victorian medicines for rheumatism and for 'cleaning
impure blood'. It is still used for inflammatory
rheumatism and arthritis, to take the heat out of flare-ups.
Interestingly, it is a natural antidote to mercury which was
a very common constituent in many Victorian (and earlier)
medicines.

REMEDIES FOR THE DIGESTION

The health and good functioning of the digestion has always been a subject of close concern to those who looked after anyone's health, given its importance in so many aspects of wellbeing. A very varied range of remedies was given for different digestive ailments—from mouth ulcers and toothache to constipation and piles. Some of the treatments used in the past are still used now, perhaps attesting to their efficacy as well as their availability. In the days before professional dentists, and even into the nineteenth century, people in rural communities may well have visited their local blacksmith for dental treatment (extractions), or they may have visited the local barber who often combined surgery (and dental work) with cutting hair. Given that treatment from either the blacksmith or the barber would have been 'robust' and painful, home treatment was often a preferable option.

This section includes treatments for:

Problems in the mouth; Stomach problems;

Constipation; Diarrhoea; and Infestations

One remedy, from Old Hartley WI, for **MOUTH ULCERS** involved applying **boracic powder** to the ulcer.

Boracic powder is derived from borax and is both antibacterial and antifungal. However, it should only be used in small quantities as it can be poisonous. Borax and boracic acid are used as a preservative for wood and as an ingredient in insecticides.

For **TOOTHACHE**:

To reduce swelling (probably from an abscess), place **salt in a stocking**, heat it and apply to the affected cheek. The heat is the key in this remedy as it will bring more blood to the area, and hopefully remove pus and debris as the blood circulation increases. Salt will help to retain the heat.

One member remembers her father using the following treatment on her when, as a little girl, she had toothache: take some **ginger powder**, wrap in a clean cloth and strap to the inside of the left wrist. Leave on overnight, and by the morning, both the toothache and the smell of ginger will have gone. The cloth was always strapped to the inside of the left wrist, regardless of which side of the mouth the toothache was.

STOMACH UPSETS

An 'upset' stomach can encompass a wide range of problems from infection to ulceration, from food sensitivity to gallbladder or liver problems. The home remedies given were purely for treating transient upsets, rather than more significant diseases.

Gregory's Powder was mentioned more than once as a treatment for an upset tummy. The powder contained ginger as well as magnesia which would help to soothe and calm an upset stomach. It was also given as a remedy for constipation and will be covered in more detail in that section.

Andrew's Liver Salts was used for upset stomachs, although it was said to work well initially but cause unpleasant problems later! The sodium bicarbonate in these salts would indeed help to neutralise too much acid in the stomach, as well as helping to release any wind there. However, it also contains magnesium sulphate (Epsom Salts) which acts as a laxative and may account for the 'unpleasant' effects later.

A remedy given by Alnwick WI told of how **Hot Ginger Wine** was given to help stomach aches. Ginger has been used for centuries to calm upset tummies and to reduce nausea, including travel sickness and morning sickness. It is a very aromatic, warming herb for the whole digestive system, helping to reduce inflammation and irritation throughout the digestive tract.

Corbridge WI gave a remedy of **Meadowsweet** as a tea to treat stomach 'discomfort'. The leaves of this beautiful plant would be made into an infusion and drunk as required.

Meadowsweet is very common in the hedgerows throughout Northumberland, flowering from July to October. As well as its traditional use for treating joint problems, it makes an excellent tea for indigestion, particularly when associated with excess acid and nausea, and provides protection for the stomach lining in cases of peptic ulcers.

A Larvin

Barley Water was a treatment given for soothing upset stomachs, as a plain, hot drink in the Winter and with sliced lemon in cooled liquid in the Spring. More information about barley can be found in the 'Tonics' section.

To Make Barley Water

2oz Pearl Barley

Cold water

Sugar, to taste

Wash the pearl barley in cold water, put in a pan and cover with cold water. Bring to the boil and boil for 5 minutes and then drain. Refill pan with 2 quarts of cold water and bring to the boil again. Simmer for about one hour. Then strain the liquid into a jug and add sugar to taste.

(Recipe from Miss E Alexander,
Old Hartley WI)

Disordered Stomach

1oz Gentian root

1 pennyworth Horehound

1 pennyworth Hiana (?) Pepper

Boil 5 quarts of water with these ingredients in it until it
boils down to 4 quarts.

Stomach Bitters

1oz Bayberry

1oz. Black Horehound

1oz Sweet Flag

1oz Ginger

Boil in 2 pints of water

Both these very interesting recipes came from an old
handwritten notebook in the possession of Mrs. Bramwell
of Horsley WI. Unfortunately, neither recipes give
dosages, but they contain very commonly used plants in
Victorian times, most of which are still in use nowadays.

WIND

Cinder Tea was a remedy mentioned several times, particularly for babies with wind. In the days when open fires and kitchen ranges were in everyone's home, it was easy to make—drop a hot cinder into a mug of water, allow to cool in the water and remove before drinking. Nowadays, charcoal tablets are available for wind and bloating.

A recipe (possibly from 1870s)

For Flatulency

6oz Peppermint

4oz Spirit of Wine

1lb Lump Sugar

Pour 3 pints of boiling water over the ingredients and then add a little gin.

(Corbridge WI)

CONSTIPATION

Known in the old herbals and medical books as 'costiveness', constipation has always been a subject close to many hearts, although not much discussed. Some of the remedies looked at in the 'Cleansing Remedies' section acted as laxatives as well.

Liquorice chunks was a favourite remedy for constipation. Whether it was the black chunks of liquorice or the commonly available sticks of liquorice root to chew, the sweetness of liquorice would make it a more palatable remedy than many others. Liquorice is often used as a sweetening agent and to disguise some of the more unpleasant-tasting medicines. It has already been mentioned as a treatment (with garlic and honey) for chesty coughs. Its use for both coughs and constipation shows the versatility of this herb. Indeed, liquorice has been used internally and topically for a range of ailments.

Liquorice can cause blood pressure to rise in some individuals, causing it to rise. Therefore, it should not be used as a regular, frequent home remedy for anyone taking blood pressure lowering medication except under professional guidance.

Senna was, and still is, a common treatment for constipation. Many proprietary brands contained senna. In the past, senna pods would be purchased from the chemist or druggist, steeped in water and then the water drunk at night.

Gregory's Powder has already been mentioned as a treatment for upset stomachs. It was also given as a remedy for constipation. The main ingredient of this proprietary powder was turkey rhubarb (*Rheum palmatum*), which has a traditional reputation as a laxative. The inclusion of ginger and magnesium in this preparation would help to relax the bowel and prevent any griping that might occur.

Rhubarb was also given as a remedy on its own in the Spring, to help clean out the digestive system. There are several species of rhubarb, most notably English rhubarb and Turkey rhubarb. Turkey rhubarb is a larger plant, more potent and powerful than the English variety and is the one used in most medicines. Turkey rhubarb comes from China and the East Indies and was given the name 'Turkey' simply to indicate that it was foreign.

Rhubarb leaves are poisonous and should not be eaten, although a traditional use was to lay the leaves on a feverish brow. Medicinally, the root is the part used either as a powder or tincture. Turkey rhubarb is considered as a main treatment for constipation, hence its appearance in a large number of laxative remedies, including Gregory's powder. However, it can cause colic and griping pains and should always be taken with a carminative such as fennel, peppermint or ginger.

Perhaps less well-known is its use to stop diarrhoea. To achieve this effect, the dose is much smaller than for its use as a laxative.

Whilst rhubarb can be a very helpful laxative for occasional constipation, it is not recommended for long term treatment as very regular use can make constipation worse.

Mrs J Jackson

Sir Jeremy Paget's Cure for Constipation

1lb Prunes

1lb Demerara Sugar

1oz Ground Ginger

1½oz powdered Senna

½ glass Brandy or 1 teaspoon whisky

Method: Stew the prunes and sugar in sufficient water to cover. Remove stones, and whilst prunes are still hot, add all the other ingredients. Stir well.

Dose: ½ a spoon at bedtime.

(Mrs J Taylor, Humshaugh WI)

(Although the size of spoon is not given, ½ a tablespoon would do the trick with this powerful recipe)

HAEMORRHOIDS

A very interesting treatment for piles (Haemorrhoids) used **Nettle leaf.**

The nettle leaves were placed in an enamel bucket, boiling water poured over and then the sufferer would sit on top of the bucket.

Nettles have a traditional use for treating piles, but this usually took the form of drinking nettle leaf tea, or applying a nettle poultice to the piles.

Nettle leaf would be particularly helpful if the piles were bleeding as nettles can help to stop bleeding.

The root has a similar action to saw palmetto in helping reduce prostate enlargement and its associated symptoms.

A Larvin

Nettles cont…

Nettles are a powerhouse of nutrition providing an extraordinary range of health benefits. The leaves contain minerals such as iron, magnesium and potassium, as well as several trace minerals and vitamins. During the war they were an important wild herb; the leaves collected for their chlorophyll content, and the stems used in paper making.

Nettle leaves make a wonderful Spring tonic because of their nutritional value, especially helpful for iron-deficiency anaemia, a common problem in the past after the winter or for women with heavy periods.

The leaf not only acts as a tonic, but also has a traditional role in cleaning the blood by helping remove acid from cells and acting as a diuretic. It is this activity that accounts for its historical use in arthritis and other joint problems, as long ago as the Romans. In treating arthritis and rheumatism, the leaf would not only be drunk as a tea, but would also be used externally as a counter-irritant. Whilst nettle is known and treated with caution for its sting, this treatment works surprisingly well.

Nettles cont...

Nettles have been, and still are, used to treat people suffering allergies such as hay fever, eczema and asthma. The leaf reduces the release of histamine, which is responsible for many of the symptoms of allergic reactions.

Often used as a vegetable in the past, nettle leaf is very similar to spinach when cooked. Only the young leaves should be used for food or for medicine as acids build up in the leaves of older plants, which can cause irritation if taken internally.

DIARRHOEA

Whether caused by an infection or due to some other cause, this was often termed 'an upset stomach'. Some of the earlier remedies given for an upset stomach would help to treat diarrhoea: meadowsweet and nettles with their astringency; ginger wine to sooth irritated or inflamed intestines; and rhubarb in small doses.

Kaolin was (and still is) a remedy used to treat diarrhoea. Often combined with morphine, it was very effective although overuse could lead to constipation.

Bilberry has been a treatment for infectious diarrhoea for centuries. Over 3000 bilberry 'stones' were found in excavations of the mediaeval hospital at Soutra Aisle near Lauder, possibly used to treat food poisoning and parasitic infections such as cryptosporidium. An effective astringent, Bilberry has also been used as a mouthwash for sore throats and bleeding gums.

Mrs B Jobling

For Diarrhoea

1 pennyworth Laudanum

1 pennyworth Spirit of Camphor

1 pennyworth Tincture of Rhubarb

1 pennyworth Peppermint

1 pennyworth Cayenne

Mix together and bottle.

Dose: 30 drops in warm water and sugar.

(Miss E Alexander, Old Hartley WI)

Another, hand-written, remedy for diarrhoea contains exactly the same ingredients, but gives quantities of each as ¼ oz, rather than 1 pennyworth. The dosage is also slightly different, being 40 drops in a wineglassful of cold water.

INFESTATION

Worm cakes were mentioned by Old Hartley WI as a treatment for worms. Unfortunately no other information was available and what exactly went into the worm cakes is not known. However, an educated guess would lead one to consider herbs such as wormwood or mugwort. Both these plants grow wild in Northumberland and both contain a bitter principle that is known to kill worms. Other constituents may well have included some form of laxative, such as senna, liquorice or rhubarb, to increase the elimination of the worms.

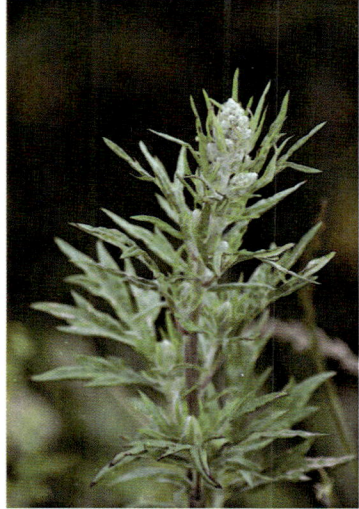

Mugwort. A Larvin

WORMS IN CHILDREN

Powdered Worm Seed   16 grains

Powdered Jalap 20 grains

Powdered Butterbur Roots 15 grains

Hyssop Powder 20 grains

Senna powder 20 grains

Mix. Give from ¼ to ½ teaspoonful every morning.

TONICS AND CLEANSERS

Spring was the traditional time to employ 'cleansing' remedies and tonics, especially on children. This aspect of home remedies has remained fresh in many members' memories, not least because the taste of some of those remedies was very unpleasant. Comments from members about being dosed with these remedies include 'willy nilly on a Monday' and 'every morning for a week'.

The concept of 'spring cleaning' the body has remained with us and is increasingly popular—although the emphasis has moved away from treating children to adults in what is now called 'detoxing'.

Cleansing the body and purifying the blood has been carried out in the Spring since at least the Middle Ages—and probably long before then. Lack of fresh fruit, vegetables and meat would have meant that the winter diet was heavily influenced by bread and starchy foods. Constipation, sluggishness and anaemia would increase during the winter. Many of the fresh plant leaves that appeared in the Spring made ideal tonics to help a sluggish digestion, as well as providing nutrients to purify and fortify the blood.

CLEANSING REMEDIES

All the 'cleansing' remedies given by WI members were for products purchased from the chemist, rather than made at home or grown or collected as plants. This, perhaps, reflects the increasing emphasis since Victorian times on patented medicines and the influence of the books of household management—such as Mrs Beeton—which were regularly published. One such book, entitled 'The New Home Encyclopaedia', published in 1932, had a section on Spring medicines which included rhubarb, sulphur mixes and a specific (constipation) recipe involving senna, manna, prunes and syrup.

The remedies given by WI members included:

Sulphur (Brimstone) and Treacle; Syrup of Figs; Epsom Salts; Lemons; Cream of Tartar

Sulphur (Brimstone) and Treacle. Given as a daily dose in the morning and usually in the Spring, several members remembered receiving this treatment, either as sulphur and treacle or brimstone and treacle. Brimstone is one of sulphur's earliest names, from an old English word meaning 'a stone that burns'. It became a popular treatment for children in Victorian times, with sulphur acting as a laxative and treacle providing iron 'to build the blood'.

Sulphur and Treacle cont...

This treatment was so well known that Charles Dickens wrote unflatteringly about it in 'Nicholas Nickleby' when Mrs Squeers dosed the pupils at Dotheboy's Hall. 'They have the brimstone and treacle, partly because if they hadn't something or other in the way of medicine they'd always be ailing... and partly because it spoils their appetites and comes cheaper than breakfast and dinner. So, it does them good and us good at the same time....'

Sulphur has already appeared as a 'First Aid' remedy in the form of magnesium sulphate paste as a drawing agent, and it is used in modern medicine in a range of preparations (especially skin treatments) for its anti-inflammatory and anti-microbial properties.

Brimstone also had other uses in the past.....

A Weight Loss Remedy

(18th Century)

Mix sugar, brimstone, egg yolk and red rose water together. Take for 20 days.

Also take powdered coltsfoot at night.

(Unfortunately, quantities are omitted from this handwritten remedy, and its efficacy is questionable.)

Epsom salts with lemon and sugar was a home remedy given in the Spring as a cleanser. Lemon and sugar were probably added to make it more palatable. The chemical name for Epsom salts is magnesium sulphate—already mentioned in the First Aid section as a drawing paste. Magnesium has also appeared as a constituent of the patented medicine, Gregory's Powders, for its laxative and calming effects. Because magnesium sulphate draws fluid, it can lead to dehydration if too much is taken internally.

Epsom salt baths are still a popular treatment in modern detoxes. It has also found use for relieving aching joints and rheumatism as magnesium is a powerful muscle relaxant, easily absorbed through the skin when soaked in hot water.

Indeed, magnesium sulphate is still used in emergency medicine nowadays to treat pre-eclampsia in pregnancy, delaying labour in pre-term births and for severe asthma.

Mrs B Jobling

Syrup of Figs was another favourite Spring cleanser. Taken as a daily morning dose, it would help to relieve constipation and 'loosen' the bowels. Figs were commonly included in many cleansing recipes.

Cream of Tartar was also mentioned as a medicine given in the Spring. This is an 'all-round' cleanser since it acts as a diuretic, emetic and as a laxative. It can be quite violent in its effect and the dose would have been carefully measured.

IRRITATION AND IMPURE BLOOD

½ oz Jamaica Sarsaparilla, ¼ oz Guaiacum Raspings,
¼ oz Liquorice Root, ¼ oz Mazerian Root,
1 oz Burdock Root, 1 oz Yellow Dock Root,
1 oz Sassafras Bark, ½ oz Brook Lime Herb

Boil for half an hour.
Take a wineglassful four times a day.

This is a typical cleansing remedy of Victorian times, including some native herbs (Burdock, Yellow Dock and Brook Lime), some herbs from the Americas, and Liquorice, which has been used in England since the Middle Ages.

TONIC REMEDIES

The tonic remedies often worked side by side with the cleansing remedies, either given separately or in combination as with Brimstone and Treacle. The principle was to first clean the body usually with laxatives, and then to build it up, with particular emphasis on the blood.

In the following section we will look at the uses and tonic properties of:

Cod Liver Oil

Virol

Barley Water

Scott's Emulsion

Rose Hip Syrup

Cinnamon

Slippery Elm

Cod Liver oil was a popular treatment for children and adults, especially during the war when it was supplied free to nursing mothers, children under 5 years old and adults over 40 years. Many children found the taste 'disgusting', even when mixed with orange juice or malt.

The oil has been popular in Northern Europe for centuries, where it has had a traditional use for stiff or aching joints and for rheumatic pains. In the nineteenth century it was a prescribed treatment to prevent rickets. Cod liver oil contains relatively high levels of Vitamin A and D, which explains some of its therapeutic benefits. More recent medical research also shows that the vitamin content helps to reduce depression especially in the winter when the body's Vitamin D levels, obtained from sunlight, fall.

Cod liver oil also provides high levels of omega 3 essential fatty acid and this has increased its popularity in recent times. The omega 3 essential fatty acid in cod liver oil is a potent anti-inflammatory, helping both the joints and the blood vessels of the circulatory system.

Cod liver oil was often mixed with malt, and malted barley was the principal ingredient of one of the most frequently mentioned tonics—Virol.

Virol was a patented product widely available from the early part of the twentieth century and was heavily advertised with slogans such as 'After Bathing, Take Virol and Milk'. One advert in 1912 proposed that Virol was recommended and prescribed by doctors all over the United Kingdom and was 'used in 500 hospitals for consumption, anaemia and rickets.' The main ingredient of Virol was malted barley, which contains iron, calcium, and several vitamins including Vitamin D and B_9 (more commonly known as Folic acid). It also contains plant sterols which have been linked to improving cardiovascular health, especially for those with diabetes or coronary heart disease. One member remembers Virol being used on babies' dummies.

As well as taking Barley in the form of malt extract, **Barley Water with lemon and sugar** was also given as a tonic drink for children in the Spring. Barley is highly nutritious, being mineral rich, containing iron and some B vitamins.

Another patented product from the chemist and given regularly to children was Scott's Emulsion.

Scott's Emulsion was variously described as 'greasy' and 'slimy' by the members who were dosed with it. It was a tonic treatment which included cod liver oil, wintergreen and hypophosphites of lime and soda. These were mixed in glycerine base. Hypophosphites of lime and of soda were common treatments in the nineteenth and early twentieth century for a range of chest conditions including asthma, tuberculosis, catarrh, whooping cough and bronchitis. Lime was also reputed to strengthen the bones and soda to increase hair growth.

Rose Hip Syrup was one of the most commonly mentioned tonic treatments. During the war, invalids and children under 5 were allocated a daily ration of Rose Hip Syrup as a source of Vitamin C due to shortages of imported fresh fruit. This particular remedy was so commonly mentioned, probably because many of the WI members were involved, as children, in the collection of rose hips as part of the war effort.

Rose Hip Syrup cont...

One member wrote: 'I remember calling the hairy white seeds inside the rose hips as 'itchy backs' which irritated the skin. But after and during the war they were a valuable source of Vitamin C and my husband collected these for Delrosa and received 3d per pound. The WI proved able organisers of this collection and those grown in the North allegedly contained more Vitamin C.' (Linda Laws, Shilbottle WI)

Although it was recognised that the hips with the highest Vitamin C content grew in the Lake District and northwards of Durham, correspondence between the Ministry of Supply and Kew Gardens felt that it was '..doubtful whether such a large quantity (2000 tons) could be obtained from these northern parts of the country' due to it being 'thinly populated, and rugged country in which roses are not very common.'

DOG ROSE

JT

Mrs J Taylor

Rose Hip Syrup cont...

Despite these fears, Northumberland was one of only three counties in 1943 who exceeded their collection target. This was put down to good organisation, all round keenness, and the presence of both *Rosa mollis* and *Rosa canina* which extended the collection season.

There are several species of wild rose in Britain, each of which have different levels of Vitamin C. Research organised by the Royal Botanic Gardens at Kew showed that some species had almost twice as much Vitamin C as others— the downy leaved dog rose (*Rosa mollis)* had almost 50% more Vitamin C than the common dog rose (*Rosa canina*). The burnet rose, with its blackish purple hips, had the lowest levels and yet was still as rich in Vitamin C as blackcurrants.

Rose hips contain many other nutrients which together have provided a strong traditional use in treating coughs and consumption, diarrhoea and dysentery, bladder stones and reducing thirst. There is, however, little Western traditional use for the most recent research from Norway and Denmark. This research indicates that the whole hips of the dog rose (*Rosa canina*) may help to reduce the pain of both osteoarthritis and rheumatoid arthritis.

Rose Hips cont…

Indeed, by reducing inflammation and working as an antioxidant, rose hips may have a much wider use, since inflammation is a significant factor in many conditions, for example cardiovascular disease, asthma and autoimmune diseases such as inflammatory bowel disease and rheumatoid arthritis.

The fine, hairy seeds within rose hips are extremely irritating in the digestive tract, and using these as part of a home remedy is not recommended.

Cinnamon in warm water was given to pupils by the matron of one school, every morning in the winter. The ground bark of the cinnamon tree has been used since the time of the Ancient Egyptians, and was once considered more precious than gold. Cinnamon has a range of medicinal uses. With a sweet, pungent taste, the powdered bark not only settles and soothes an upset stomach, but also acts as a very effective antiseptic in the urinary tract, combating both the bacterium *E.coli* and the fungus *Candida albicans*. Cinnamon also stimulates cognitive ability, improving mental function and alertness. More recent research indicates that it has a role to play in lowering blood cholesterol, reducing blood sugar levels and increasing insulin production.

Cinnamon cont…

Mrs J Jackson

Slippery Elm Powder was a convalescent treatment recounted by one member of Berwick WI who remembers her mother using it within the family for those recovering from illness. The powdered inner bark of the Slippery Elm tree makes a highly nutritious, soothing and gentle gruel when mixed with water or milk. Suitable for both adults and children, it soothes and protects the lining of the digestive tract and helps weight gain following illness. This protective property makes it suitable for use in any ulceration or inflammation in the digestive tract —from reflux and heartburn to colitis and irritable bowel syndrome.

MISCELLANEOUS HOME REMEDIES

In this section there are a range of remedies for health problems ranging from the eyes to the skin, from headaches to treatments specifically for women. Some of the ingredients of the treatments have already been mentioned in other sections, some are very specific.

Eyes

Skin and Hair

Headaches

Women's Treatments

Kidney and Bladder Treatments

Insomnia

A Cancer 'Cure'

EYES

To heal an ulcer on the eye lid, **tea leaves** were used to bathe the eyelid. Unfortunately, we do not know whether the leaves themselves or an infusion of the leaves was used. However, it is most likely that a strong infusion would be used as an eyebath.

Two remedies were given for treating styes:

Salt Water to bathe the affected eye lid.

Marshmallow Leaf Infusion for bathing the eyelid. This remedy was given to a member by an herbalist in Carlisle in the early 1950's. Traditionally, the root and leaf of mallow and marshmallow have been used interchangeably as medicines, although the root is considered more powerful. Whichever part is used, it is a very soothing treatment for any kind of irritation (internal or external), whether for sore throats or dry, irritating coughs, for itchy and chapped skin, or for an inflamed, ulcerated digestive tract. Culpeper advocated its use to treat fevers, by infusing mallow with fennel and parsley. The root was a traditional treatment for teething babies. The root would be cleaned and peeled and, in the same way as rusks, the baby would chew on the root.

SKIN

Acne, spots, eczema, psoriasis and other skin complaints are highly visible problems that can cause much unhappiness, and for some, lasting skin damage or scarring. Causes are various from hormonal to digestive; from immune system dysregulation to diet. Likewise, treatments vary depending on the cause.

For a chickenpox boil, a member of Ulgham WI remembers the use of a hot **starch poultice.** Norham WI recounted the use of a **stocking , filled with salt and heated** to treat the swellings of mumps.

ACNE

To prevent spots or acne, eat a **boiled onion** once a week, every week.

To treat acne, apply a **cabbage leaf poultice** to the affected area. Cabbage leaf has already been mentioned for its use in reducing swelling for sprains, and joint problems. If there were only one or two spots, this could be a practical treatment, but if there were more, there would probably be greater benefit in eating the cabbage to cleanse the digestive system.

ECZEMA

One member remembers a treatment given by an herbalist in Ovington of a poultice of **bramble and elder leaves.** In the same way that tea leaves contain tannins which can protect irritated or sore skin, so too do bramble and elder leaves. Such a poultice would be helpful for eczema which was sore, irritated and red.

Mrs B Jobling

Another treatment given for skin complaints in general was the use of **Epsom Salts** in the bath. The bath to be as hot as possible, and to last for twenty minutes, after which, pat the skin dry and stay warm in bed.

SORE SKIN, CHAPPED SKIN;
HACKS & KEENS

Sore and chapped skin, and chilblains were a common problem in the days before central heating. A book written in 1610 by an Edward Potter, doctor and surgeon of Tynemouth warns at the beginning of his book 'warm not thy legges at the fire'. No doubt, to avoid chilblains.

Snowfire ointment was remembered by several members for sore, chapped skin and for chilblains. It was bought as a solid stick from the chemist and, when warmed, a small amount would melt and be rubbed into the afflicted area. It is still made and available. The base of this ointment is paraffin wax which provides a protective coating to the skin and chlorophyll which gives it its green colour. Other ingredients include Oils of citronella, thyme, clove and cade (an oil derived from a relative of the Juniper bush).

Wintergreen Ointment was remembered for its use on hacks and keens, although it has also been used for chapped skin and chilblains too. Wintergreen is a ground-hugging shrub whose leaves provide a volatile oil containing high levels of methyl salicylate, a close relative of salicylic acid.

Wintergreen Ointment continued…

This volatile oil is used in a range of medicines, chewing gums and toothpastes, both for flavouring and for its medicinal properties. Methyl salicylate is used for pain relief and to reduce inflammation in rheumatism, stiff or painful joints, neuralgia and chapped hands.

This ointment is still available, both as wintergreen ointment and as methyl salicylate ointment. However, methyl salicylate ointment is likely, nowadays, to be produced from synthetically prepared methyl salicylate.

CHILBLAINS

As well as the Snowfire and Wintergreen ointments mentioned, another remembered remedy for chilblains was **urine.** This was a remedy from the 1950's and the affected part (usually on the foot or heel) would be immersed in a potty.

Urine therapy is still used in Traditional Chinese and Ayurvedic medicine, and in some therapies in the West. External treatments for which urine has been popular include wound cleaning and as ear and nose drops.

HEADLICE

Head lice have been living with man since the earliest times. Although the 'nit nurse' no longer visits schools, there are several proprietary shampoos now available and, of course, the 'nit comb'.

One member remembers the use of **Quassia water** as a hair rinse to kill the head lice. The bark of the Quassia tree would be boiled in water to make a decoction, strained and the resulting liquor used to rinse the head.

The Quassia tree originates in the Far East, where it was used 'as a secret remedy in the malignant endemic fevers which frequently prevailed in Surinam'. The secret of this wood was bought by a Swede, Daniel Rolander in 1756 who brought the tree to Europe. The bark was the part used medicinally and it was considered, at one time, to be an effective and cheaper alternative to cinchona bark (quinine) for the treatment of malaria.

The bark is intensely bitter and, like many of the very bitter plants such as wormwood, this property is responsible for its worm and parasite killing activity.

HEADACHES

A headache was described simply as a 'pain in the head' in old herbals. Nowadays, we have a range of descriptions for headaches—for example, tension, cluster, migraine. They can be caused by various triggers such as stress or tension, food, weather, hormones, bright light or eyestrain.

Vinegar was used as a treatment for headaches, with a cloth or brown paper soaked in vinegar placed over the forehead. Vinegar has already been mentioned as a cooling treatment for sunburn and this use, for headaches, works on the same principle.

Peppermint oil and Peppermint Tea were two traditional remedies used to treat headaches. Peppermint has a cooling effect, both on the skin and internally and so would have worked in a similar way to vinegar.

For migraine headaches, **Feverfew** was, and still is, used as a treatment. One member of Norham WI has successfully used an infusion of the leaf for the past fifteen years for both headaches and migraines. She finds it works within thirty minutes.

Feverfew cont...

However, another member, from Berwick WI, has used feverfew capsules to no great effect. This difference in efficacy highlights the fact that no single medicine works for everyone—and plant medicine is no different.

According to Culpeper, feverfew 'is very effectual for all pains in the head coming of a cold cause..also for the Vertigo'. It is the description of 'a cold cause' that is possibly significant since feverfew has been shown to work better where migraine, and vertigo or tinnitus are present and for migraines which respond better to warmth than to cold, and where it is also associated with nausea and vomiting.

A small study in 1985 at the City of London Migraine Clinic tested the effects of feverfew on seventeen patients who were already using this herb. Nine patients were randomly given (unknowingly) a placebo capsule. The results showed that those given the placebo had an increase in frequency and severity of their migraines and an increase in nausea and vomiting.

Feverfew continued…

Feverfew leaf is intensely bitter, and this accounts for its unpleasant taste for some, as well as one of its traditional uses to kill worms in the digestive tract.

The fresh leaf can cause dermatitis and/or mouth and gastric ulceration in those sensitive to the Daisy family.

A Larvin

REMEDIES for WOMEN

Home remedies for 'women's troubles' have always been one of the more limited areas of information. Older herbals talked of a condition called 'hysteria' in relation to gynaecological problems. This was based on the belief that many nervous disorders arose from the womb.

One of the possible reasons that home remedies for women are not so well documented is the former, unofficial use of herbs to procure abortions - a criminal offence. Since some of the herbs used to treat period problems could equally be used to bring about an abortion, this would be talked of in private and quietly.

Pregnancy gave the widest range of remembered remedies:

Goose grease was a remedy used to reduce or avoid stretch marks during pregnancy. Although more commonly known as a home remedy for chesty coughs and colds, many older ointment remedies used goose grease as a base. Goose fat not only provided energy as a food, but also provided the fat soluble vitamins (Vitamins A, D, E and K). It is, perhaps, this vitamin content together with the emollient effects of the fat that helped to reduce stretch marks.

Raspberry leaf tea was mentioned both for labour pains and as a drink to be taken during pregnancy. An infusion of the leaves was used as a uterine tonic, to strengthen the muscles of the uterus, which would then help an easier delivery. However, if taken too early in pregnancy (before the last trimester), it may cause miscarriage. The leaf contains reasonable amounts of tannins which accounts for its traditional use in treating diarrhoea.

Mrs J Jackson

Lady's Mantle was mentioned to reduce heavy periods. This beautiful plant is found both in the wild and cultivated in gardens. It takes its common name from the fact that women used to apply the leaves to their breasts to recover their form after giving birth and lactation. Lady's Mantle has a long usage as a wound herb, allaying bleeding. Culpeper describes it as 'one of the most singular wound herbs that is'. It is this plant's ability to stop bleeding that led to its use for women with heavy periods.

Mrs J Taylor

KIDNEY AND WATER INFECTIONS

It is not surprising that many old herbals give a vast range of plants to treat 'the gravel, stranguary or stones'. These would be extremely painful conditions, as Samuel Pepys knew well. However, the alternative to plant medicine was surgery, with a lack of anaesthesia and the very real, common dangers of infection. Herbal diuretics were the most commonly employed treatments, including pellitory at the wall, parsley, wild carrot, and radish.

Sir John Hill writes of the radish 'the juice of the roots, freshly gathered, with a little white wine is an excellent remedy against the gravel… Scarce anything operates more speedily by urine, or brings away little stones more successfully'.

PELLITORY AT THE WALL

JT

member of the nettle family.

Mrs J Taylor

Parsley tea was a remedy given for treating kidney complaints. All parts of parsley— the leaf, root and seed— have been and still are used for kidney complaints and to treat arthritis. An infusion of the leaf would be used to make a tea, the root would be cooked and eaten rather like a parsnip and the seeds would be steeped in wine to make a tincture. Parsley tea was used in the First World War in the trenches to reduce kidney complications from dysentery. The traditional uses for Parsley are very varied, from settling colic and expelling wind to breaking down kidney stones and relieving jaundice.

Barley Water was given as a treatment for water infections. Pearl barley is the grain without its outer skin and this is the form used to make a decoction for water infections. A barley water decoction would contain high levels of mucilage which would be very soothing for irritation and inflammation in the bladder.

REMEDIES for INSOMNIA

The causes of insomnia are as varied as the many folk remedies available. Whether the problem is not being able to fall asleep at bedtime or waking during the night, it can affect both health and quality of life. Laudanum (opium) was the treatment of choice in Victorian times even for children, and was readily available from chemist shops.

Lettuce sandwiches were one of the more common home remedies, although the cultivated garden lettuce has fewer sedative properties than the wild lettuce, and a large amount would need to be consumed to have an appreciable effect.

Today, a range of herbal remedies are available over-the-counter, which contain herbs such as valerian, passionflower and hops to promote sleep.

Mrs J Taylor

VALERIAN

JT

Hot Milk and Honey was recommended as a remedy to help insomnia. This is a very traditional treatment whose efficacy can now be explained by science. Milk (and all dairy products) contain an amino acid called tryptophan which is essential for the production of the hormone serotonin. Serotonin contributes to relaxation and a feeling of well-being. Tryptophan works more quickly in the presence of sugar—hence the benefit of adding honey to the milk. However, if one is intolerant of dairy products, this can have the opposite effect and be a factor in causing insomnia in the first place!

Continuing with the same theme, **Boily** was a traditional bedtime treat for children. Made from bread, milk and sugar it would be both comforting and calming.

Boily - milk, sugar & white bread.

Mrs J Taylor

A **Lavender pillow** was given as a remedy for insomnia, using either lavender flowers on their own, or mixed with lemon balm leaves. The scent of lavender flowers is, indeed, calming and relaxing which can help one fall asleep more easily. A **lavender sponge bath** was also recommended to soothe a bedridden patient. As with many herbs (and scents), there are two sides to their efficacy. Whilst small amounts of lavender scent will help to relax and induce sleep, larger amounts can serve to stimulate and keep one awake. As Culpeper wrote ' the chemical oil drawn from lavender, usually called oil of spike, is of so fierce and piercing a quality, that it is cautiously to be used, some few drops being sufficient'...

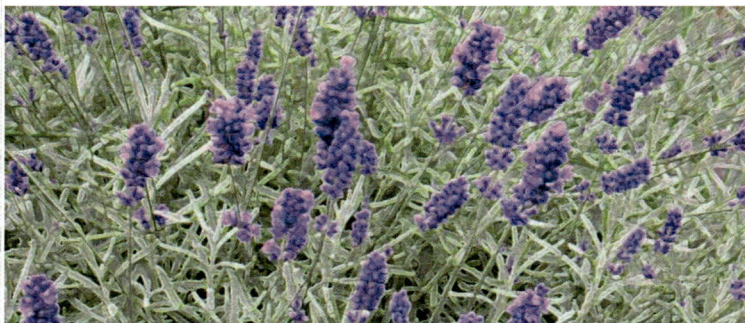

A Larvin

MISCELLANEOUS

A 'Cure' for Cancer

½ oz citrus of potash

½ oz radio phosphate of potash dissolved in a pint of
water, forming 20 fluid oz. solution.

Take ½ oz twice daily in water.

(Mrs J Taylor, Humshaugh WI)

THE STILL ROOM

The Still Room was the domain of women. Whether it was a separate room in a large house, with perhaps a Still Room Maid, or whether it was the kitchen in a smaller house, the Still Room was where food and medicines were prepared and stored. Receipt books (Recipe books) would have been used for those who could read and write and it was from here that the Lady of the Manor would have dispensed medicines and advice to the poorer people in her community.

As towns and cities developed and more people were able to read and write, so the number of personal recipe books increased. Newspapers from the eighteenth century included details of 'miraculous' cures and remedies, with testimonials, which were cut out or copied out and placed in these home recipe books. Whether they were ever used in the home is, in most cases, not known .

In rural communities, what is striking is the way that some recipes and plants were used interchangeably for people and animals, especially cows and horses.

One member of Berwick WI told of gypsies coming to her parents' farm and using what was called the 'health plant' to treat joint problems in both adults and horses. Unfortunately, we do not know which plant this was.

Similarly, in home notebooks, treatments for adults and children would be found side by side with treatments for animals. One member, from Horsley WI, has a handwritten remedy book which has just this—so, next to a corn and wart treatment is a 'cure for warble fly' and a recipe for colds is followed by a prescription for 'A Conditioning Powder for Horses'.

As more people learned to read and write, the number of pamphlets, booklets and health management books increased. Since this took place mainly during the nineteenth century, many of these recipes contained fewer plants and more 'chemicals' or manufactured products such as paregoric elixir (a tincture of opium with camphor), vitriol (sulphuric acid), carbolic acid and even mercury—all for internal use. Laudanum (another form of opium) was also a very common ingredient in the recipes.

Despite the increasing presence of minerals and chemicals in these recipes, plants still had an important role in most of them. However, the range of plants in these recipes tended to be more 'exotic' than 'local', perhaps highlighting the point made by a Dr Cullen in 1812 who suggested that the 'extraordinary commendations' ascribed to quassia bark arose as much from 'the partiality shown to new medicines' as its efficacy. 'Exotics' were those plants brought to this country from the growth of empire and new trade routes from Central, South and North America, the West and East Indies, India, and China and included sarsaparilla (from South and Central America), jalap (from the West Indies), and cascara (from North America).

Patented medicines (such as the wonderfully named 'Rush's Thunderbolt' - a very powerful laxative pill made from jalap and mercury) were increasingly available and popular from chemists and druggists. So much so, that books were written with recipes of approximate formulas for these medicines.

Wines, syrups, cordials, beers and vinegars were popular remedies made in the Still Room and the home. The original reason for making medicines in this way was to preserve the herbs since alcohol is a useful preservative, as is vinegar and, to a lesser extent, sugar.

Herb wines were essentially no different from the modern day tincture medicines which are simply the liquor produced from herbs steeped in alcohol and water. Herb wines were probably more palatable because of their sugar content. Although no recipes were given for wines, two particular plants were mentioned as being made into wines within the home — cowslip wine and burnet wine.

Cowslips have long been a traditional treatment for coughs, having a soothing and sedative effect which made it very suitable for children. It was also used 'to bring out the rash' in measles.

COWSLIP

Mrs J Taylor

JT

121

Whether the burnet wine was made from greater burnet (*Sanguisorba officinalis*) or salad burnet (*Pimpinella saxifraga*), whether the leaf or root was used, is not known. Either or both may have been used. Culpeper writes of the greater burnet 'this is a most precious herb; the continual use of it preserves the body in health, and the spirits in vigour', whereas William Turner (a famous sixteenth century botanist, cleric and doctor from Morpeth) advised the use of salad burnet infused in wine for the cure of gout and rheumatism.

Cordials and syrups were pleasant ways to preserve fruits as medicines. We have already seen a range of fruit and vegetable syrups being used for respiratory infections. Honey was often substituted for sugar, which would confer additional medicinal and health benefits.

Elderflowers were a popular ingredient for cordials, not only for their fragrance, but also for their medicinal value in treating coughs and colds, fevers, and allergies such as hay fever and eczema. The flowers were also highly prized for cosmetic purposes, as they were believed to whiten the skin and help remove freckles.

Elderflower Cordial

8 large heads of elderflower

1Kg sugar

1 tablespoon wine vinegar

16 pints water

1 large lemon, cut and squeezed

Method: Stir all ingredients together and leave for 24 hours. Strain and bottle.

(Alnwick WI)

Elderflowers were recommended by the Ministry of Food, during the war, as a deliciously fragrant alternative to Muscatel wine.

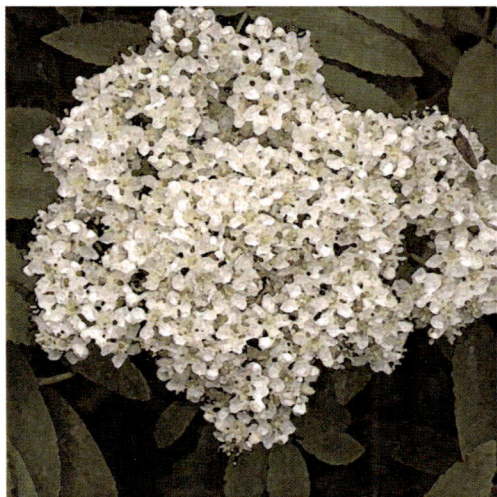

A Larvin

ROSE HIP SYRUP

There are many, varied recipes for making rose hip syrup. Most recipes call for two or three infusions of the rose hips, with the resulting liquors being combined and then boiled for a short time with sugar (or honey) in the ratio of 1 part liquor to 1 part sugar. It is really as simple as that.

Tips:

- Collect hips after the first frosts, when they are softer.
- Top and tail the hips before use.
- If you cannot mince them, boil the hips for about 5 minutes and then mash.
- Use the finest possible weave of muslin for straining, as the hairs are very irritating to the digestive tract and need to be removed from the liquor. If necessary, strain two or more times.
- Use small bottles to store the syrup, as it only lasts a few days once opened. Keep refrigerated.

A War-time Recipe from the Ministry of Food

Rose Hip Syrup

2lbs Rose hips

3 pints boiling water and 1½ pints boiling water

1¼lbs Sugar

Method: Mince rose hips coarsely and put into pan in which 3 pints of water are boiling. Remove from heat and leave for 15 minutes. Strain through a flannel or crash jelly bag. Return residue of hips to saucepan, add 1½ pints of boiling water, stir, remove from heat and allow to stand for 10 minutes. Strain this liquor as before. Add the 2 liquors together and strain again (to ensure no small hairs from hips are present). Boil down the combined liquors until the juice measures about 1½ pints. Add the sugar and boil for 5 minutes. Pour into hot, sterile bottles and seal immediately.

VINEGARS

Vinegar, made from apples (for apple cider vinegar) or grapes (for wine vinegar) is an excellent tonic for the entire digestive system. It assists the body to regulate its acid/alkaline balance, hence its use for arthritis and rheumatism. Being a food high in minerals, especially potassium, the addition of fruit to a vinegar provides additional nutrients such as vitamins.

Blackberry Vinegar

Blackberries

Malt Vinegar

Sugar

Method: Place 1lb of blackberries in a dish and cover with malt vinegar. Cover dish with cloth and leave for 24 hours. Then sieve through muslin, into a saucepan. Add 1 lb sugar to each pint of vinegar/juice and boil until syrup forms. (Keep removing any scum that forms on the top). Pour into sterilised bottles and seal well.

This can last up to 3 years unopened.

(Acomb WI)

Raspberry Vinegar

2 quarts Fresh Raspberries

2 quarts Vinegar

Sugar

Pour the vinegar over the raspberries and leave to stand in a covered vessel for 4 days. Stir every morning. Strain, then add 1lb of sugar to every pint of juice. Bring slowly to the boil and simmer for 20 minutes.

Bottle when cold and cork tightly for winter use.

Blackcurrants and blackberries can also be used.

When required for treatment of colds, dilute with hot water.

(Mrs Pat Goff, Berwick WI)

Raspberry, Blackcurrant
and Blackberry Vinegar

1½lbs of mixed fruit
1 pint vinegar
1lb loaf sugar to each pint of liquid

Method: Place fruit and vinegar in a bowl and crush the fruit. Leave to soak for 2 days. Strain the juice off and to every pint of liquid add 1lb of loaf sugar. Put into a pan and simmer gently for 20 minutes. When quite cold, bottle.

It will keep any length of time and is invaluable in hot water for colds and chest infections.

Mrs J Taylor

CREAMS AND OINTMENTS

Creams and ointments were often made at home. With few, if any, preservatives, they would need to be used quickly and then replenished. Both creams and ointments would have herbs—flowers, chopped leaves or decoctions of roots— added during the process and then either left in or strained.. The herbs used would depend on the purpose for which the cream was made. For example, calendula flower or comfrey leaf for an healing cream; chickweed herb, lavender flowers or plantain leaves for a soothing cream; nettle leaf for an astringent ointment for piles.

Ointments are usually a mix of fat or wax (such as beeswax, goose fat or lard) and an oil. The simplest form of ointment is goose fat or lard—on its own or with herbs added.

A cream involves mixing water with an oil (in much the same way as making mayonnaise), with the addition of an 'emulsifier' such as beeswax or lanolin to distribute the oil evenly throughout the cream. Herbs would be added during the process.

A Comfrey Salve

For Scratches and Bruises

Ingredients:

>2 cups good quality Olive Oil
>
>1 oz (approx. 2 tablespoons) fresh Comfrey leaves
>
>1 oz (approx 2 tablespoons) fresh Lavender flowers
>
>1 oz (approx 2 tablespoons) fresh calendula flowers
>
>½ cup beeswax

Method:

- Gently warm the olive oil and herbs in the top of a double boiler for about 30 minutes. Stir frequently. It should 'bubble' a bit at the edges, but not throughout the mixture.

- Strain the oil through a strainer. Reserve the oil and discard the herbs.

- Melt the beeswax in the top of the double boiler. When fully melted, remove from the heat and add the strained oil. Stir until completely blended.

- Pour the mixture into jars of salve tins.

- Once it is cool, label and date your salve.

Hints:

If fresh herbs are not available, use dried herbs, but use only half the quantity given for fresh herbs.

Grate the beeswax before melting it.

A Hand Lotion

4oz Glycerine
¼oz (Gum) Tragacanth
½ pint Boiling Water (Soft, if possible)
6 drops Lavender essence

Method: Put the tragacanth into a bowl and pour on the boiling water. Leave the bowl handy and stir frequently for 2 hours or until dissolved. When cool, add glycerine and essence (and colouring, if liked). Put into sterilised jars and leave until cold, then seal.

A Hand Cream
For Sores and Bruises

1lb Lard
Handful of Wormwood, Elderflowers
and Groundsel

Method: Simmer the herbs in the lard for thirty minutes. Strain through muslin or fine sieve and pot.

(Corbridge WI)

To Clean Hands

Melt lard and allow to cool. Before it is set, add sugar, mix and pot. Use to clean hands, especially after gardening.

(Bolam Park WI)

HAIR PREPARATIONS

Before the advent of the huge, sometimes mind-boggling, variety of shampoos, conditioners, scalp cleansers, hair restorers, hair washing and rinsing tended to be a much simpler affair. This is not to say that people were any less concerned about their appearance. Hair rinses, in particular, elicited a variety of herbal infusions:

Nettle leaf infusion was used on dark hair to give it a shine.

Vinegar was recommended to remove grease from the hair.

Chamomile flower infusion was used on fair hair.

Rosemary leaf infusion was used to strengthen the hair.

Soap spirit was recommended to remove hair lacquer and to clean the scalp.

A Roman remedy to reduce hair loss involved making an ointment from cabbage leaf and rubbing into the scalp

A recipe to promote hair growth was given as...

> Equal quantities of Olive Oil and spirit of Rosemary;
> and add a few drops of oil of nutmeg.
> Mix and rub roots of hair every night.

HOUSEHOLD and
GARDEN REMEDIES

Making household remedies was also the responsibility of the woman of the house, who often prepared her own polishes, disinfectants and cleaners.

Powdered Borax, sprinkled in the room, was recommended to kill insects. This also helped to deodorise a room.

Charcoal (in a paper bag) was also used to deodorise and freshen a room.

Horse chestnuts were used as an alternative to camphor as mothballs.

Sweet Cicely seeds were a traditional polish for wooden furniture. The seeds, crushed and powdered, would be rubbed onto the wood both to polish and to scent it.

To destroy flies, soak 1oz of **quassia chips** overnight in a pint of water. The following day, bring to the boil and boil for 10 minutes. When cold, place in small saucers or dishes in the rooms.

To keep away flies, hang a bunch of **clover blossoms** in a room.

A bed made from **Yew wood** would deter bugs.

HOUSEHOLD and
GARDEN REMEDIES

IN THE GARDEN

Rhubarb leaves, infused and the liquid used as an insecticide. Since the leaves are poisonous to man, it is likely that they will also be poisonous to some insects.

Comfrey Leaves, soaked in water will produce an effective fertiliser for the soil, high in nitrogen but with a very strong smell.

From a notebook of 1796, the benefits of the **Elder tree** in the garden were given as...

- Saving turnip from fly
- Preserving fruit trees from blight
- Preserving cabbage plants from caterpillars.

Dwarf elder was deemed to be the most potent of the elder trees and that the leaves should be thrown over the ground or the fruit trees struck with the elder twigs.

INDEX OF REMEDIES AND AILMENTS

INDEX OF REMEDIES AND AILMENTS

INDEX OF REMEDIES AND AILMENTS

INDEX OF REMEDIES AND AILMENTS